Man in the Universe

SOME CONTINUITIES
IN INDIAN THOUGHT

MAN IN THE UNIVERSE

Some Continuities in Indian Thought

W. NORMAN BROWN

UNIVERSITY OF CALIFORNIA PRESS
Berkeley and Los Angeles 1966

University of California Press
Berkeley and Los Angeles, California
Cambridge University Press
London, England

Library of Congress Catalog Card Number 66–12648
Printed in the United States of America

The Rabindranath Tagore
Memorial Lectureship

was established in 1961, the centenary of the Nobel Prize-winning poet of India, to honor the life and work of a man whose contributions to arts and letters were of universal significance, although expressed in terms reflecting his own culture. The annual lectures are devoted to major themes relating to Indian civilization.

The Lectureship is administered by a committee of the Association for Asian Studies, and is composed of members drawn from the sponsoring universities: Columbia University, Harvard University, University of California, Berkeley, University of Chicago, University of Michigan, University of Pennsylvania, and University of Wisconsin. Richard L. Park of the University of Pittsburgh is secretary of the committee.

1964–1965
PATRONS

Mr. and Mrs. Harvey Breit
The Association for Asian Studies, Inc.
The University of Michigan, Committee
on South and Southeast Asian Studies

Host University: *The University of Michigan*
Chairman: *O. L. Chavarria-Aguilar*

Preface

The fourth series of the Rabindranath Tagore Memorial Lectures was presented by Professor W. Norman Brown of the University of Pennsylvania during March, 1965, on the campus of The University of Michigan. The theme of the Lectures constituted an appropriate tribute to the wise and humane man in whose honor the Lectureship was established. Publication of Professor Brown's Lectures makes available to a wider audience profound and original contributions to the study of Indian religion and philosophy that were enthusiastically received by those fortunate enough to hear them in Ann Arbor.

W. Norman Brown occupies a unique position in Indian studies both in this country and abroad. He is a scholar of international stature. His devotion to Sanskrit and to Indology, in the broadest sense, is of somewhat more than half a century's standing. His interests are catholic and wide-ranging, and his many contributions to the field give ample evidence of his disciplined scholarship. He is as concerned with India's present as he is with her remote past. This dual concern has borne fruit in the establishment of the American Institute of Indian Studies (Philadelphia and Poona) for which Professor Brown, its first President, has been largely responsible. Indian studies in the United States today—from Vedic religion to contemporary social problems, from Indic philology to Carnatic music—are vigorous and prospering, largely because of the attention, the vision, and the tenacity of W. Norman Brown. As teacher and scholar, as administrator and inspirer, he has touched the lives of a great many of us.

Professor Brown has been the recipient of many honors. He is past President of both the American Oriental Society and of the Association for Asian Studies; he has been elected President of the XXVIIth International Congress of Orientalists, to which The University of Michigan will be privileged to be host in August, 1967. He has been awarded honorary degrees by the University of Madras in 1957, the University of Pennsylvania in 1963, and The University of Michigan in 1965. In 1961 the Sanskrit College of Calcutta conferred upon him the title of *Jñāna Ratnākara* ("Ocean of Learning") .

The subject of the 1964–1965 Tagore Memorial Lectures centers on the challenging, continually fascinating question of man's relation to his fellow man and to his universe, and on one people's answer to these persisting questions. By way of introduction, and at the author's own suggestion, the Lectures are preceded by "The Content of Cultural Continuity in India," Professor Brown's Presidential Address to the thirteenth annual meeting of the Association for Asian Studies in Chicago, May 28, 1961.

For Professor Brown's lectures, a debt of gratitude is acknowledged to the Committee for the Rabindranath Tagore Memorial Lectureship and to its Secretary, Dean Richard L. Park of the University of Pittsburgh; to the Association for Asian Studies, Inc., and to Mr. and Mrs. Harvey Breit of New York.

For indispensable and unstinting aid in connection

with local arrangements for the fourth series of lectures, I am grateful to Professor L. A. Peter Gosling, Director of the Center for South and Southeast Asian Studies, The University of Michigan; to Mrs. Victoria Harper of the Association for Asian Studies; and to President Harlan H. Hatcher and the then Vice-President Roger W. Heyns, who so graciously extended the hospitality of The University of Michigan to Professor and Mrs. Brown.

Not the least debt is due the Lecturer himself, whose *śiṣya,* for an all-too-brief three years, I was—and indeed still am.

O. L. CHAVARRIA-AGUILAR
The University of Michigan

ABBREVIATIONS FOR WORKS FREQUENTLY QUOTED

AV	Atharva Veda
BAU	Bṛhadāraṇyaka Upanishad
BG	Bhagavad Gītā
CU	Chāndogya Upanishad
Īśā	Īśā Upanishad
Kena	Kena Upanishad
KU	Kaṭha Upanishad
Maitri	Maitri Upanishad
Māṇḍ	Māṇḍukya Upanishad
Muṇḍ	Muṇḍaka Upanishad
RV	Rig Veda
Śvet	Śvetāśvatara Upanishad
Tait	Taittirīya Upanishad

Contents

INTRODUCTION

The Content of Cultural Continuity in India

One of the problems recurring in the Buddhist Pali Texts is the question of what it is that transmigrates. Buddhism accepts as axiomatic the doctrine of rebirth, a process of "renewal of becomings" until the attainment of complete knowledge, whereupon the process terminates. At the same time, the Pali texts are committed to the doctrine that there is no soul. The two doctrines, held simultaneously, presented a difficulty of which the Buddhist monks were well aware. If there is no soul, no Ego, no self, and yet rebirth is a fact, what is reborn?

Of the many passages bearing upon the parts of this problem, one of the best known is that in which the Venerable Nāgasena expounds the No-Soul doctrine to King Milinda. Nāgasena had remarked to the king that, though he was called Nāgasena, this was merely a convenient designation, an appellation, and any other designation would have done as well. There was no essential Nāgasena, no Ego Nāgasena.

This was more than the king could understand. "If there is no Ego," he objected, "who furnishes you monks

The Presidential address delivered at the thirteenth annual meeting of the Association for Asian Studies in Chicago on March 28, 1961. Reprinted from the *Journal of Asian Studies,* XX (August, 1961), 427–434.

with robes, medicine, and your other needs, who uses these things? Who observes the precepts, who undertakes meditation, who does evil? Without an Ego there can be no merit, no demerit; good and evil deeds can have no fruit. There can be no teacher. When you tell me that your fellow monks address you as Nāgasena, what is this Nāgasena? Is the hair of your head Nāgasena?" "No, your majesty!" "The hair of your body?" "No!" "The nails, skin, teeth?" and he catalogued some thirty parts of the body. "Is it form, sensation, perception, the predispositions, consciousness, or all of them together, or something besides them?" Always the answer was "No." Then the king said to Nāgasena, "You are telling me a lie. There is no Nāgasena."

In reply to the king, Nāgasena resorted to a parable, using as its subject the chariot in which the king said he came to Nāgasena's presence. "What is this chariot?" asked Nāgasena. "Is it the pole, or the axle, or the wheels, or the chariot-body, or the banner-staff, or the yoke, or the reins, or the goad, or all of them together?" Each time the king answered, "No." "Then," said Nāgasena, "king though you are, you are lying to me. There is no chariot!" Thus refuted, the king denied that he had lied, and then conceded that the word "chariot" was only a term, an appellation, a convenient designation, a name for all the parts mentioned. "Similarly," pointed out Nāgasena, "must you understand the word 'Nāgasena.' It is but an appellation, a convenient designation. But in the absolute sense there is no Nāgasena to be found here." [1]

Later, in the same text, King Milinda asked Nāgasena the question which naturally followed: "If there is no Ego, what is it that is born in the next existence?"

"Your majesty," replied Nāgasena, "it is name and form that is born in the next existence." By "name and form" (*nāmarūpa*) the Pali means "individuality." Yet the individuality in the next existence, Nāgasena went on to explain, is not the same individuality as that in this existence; "But with the individuality of this existence, your majesty, one does a deed—it may be good or it may be wicked—and by reason of this deed another individuality is born into the next existence."

"Reverend sir," asked the king, "if it is not the same individuality that is born into the next existence, is not one freed from one's evil deeds?"

"If one were not born into another existence," answered Nāgasena, "one would be freed from one's evil deeds; but, your majesty, inasmuch as one is born into another existence, therefore is one not freed from one's evil deeds."

Still puzzled, King Milinda asked for an illustration, and Nāgasena gave him several, including the following:

"Your majesty, it is as if a man were to buy from a cowherd a pot of milk, and were to leave it with the cowherd, and go off, thinking he would come the next day and take it. And on the next day it were to turn into sour cream; and the man were to come back, and say, 'Give me the pot of milk.' And the other were to show him the sour cream; and the first man were to say, 'I did not buy sour cream from you. Give me the pot of milk.' And the cowherd were to say, 'While you were gone, your milk turned into sour cream;' and they, quarrelling, were to come to you. Whose cause, your majesty, would you sustain?"

"That of the cowherd, reverend sir."

"And why?"

"Because, in spite of what the man might say, the one sprang from the other."

"In exactly the same way, your majesty, although the individuality which is born into the next existence is different from the individuality which is to end at death, nevertheless, it is sprung from it. Therefore is one not freed from one's evil deeds?" [2]

In other passages the simile of milk is extended to include the successive transformations into sour cream, butter, or ghee. The texts illustrate the point that there is continuity and causal connection, though not identity, of individuality.

And now arises a third question: what causes individuality to be reborn? In the Buddhist doctrine of the Chain of Dependent Origination, individuality is said to depend upon consciousness (Pali, *viññāna;* Sanskrit, *vijñāna*), and the Buddha is represented as saying in the Mahānidānasutta of the Dīgha Nikāya, "Were consciousness not to descend in the maternal womb, name and form, that is individuality, would not consolidate in the maternal womb." And he goes on to say that were consciousness to be severed from a child, name and form would not attain growth, increase, and development. "Accordingly," says he, "we have in consciousness the occasion, the origin, and the dependence of individuality. . . . Verily this individuality coupled with consciousness is all there is to be born, or to grow old, or to die, or to leave one existence, or to spring up in another. It is all that is meant by any affirmation, predication, or declaration we may make concerning anybody. It constitutes knowledge's field of action. And it is all that is reborn to appear in its present shape."[3] In short, we can see that consciousness is the only invariable, the one unalterable element, in the Pali Buddhist doctrine of rebirth.

I have used this bit of Buddhist doctrinal exposition because it presents a figurative analogy to the history of civilized man in India. Since the third millennium B.C.

India has had a highly developed civilization, and we can see that this has had a continuity through successive periods with many variations from then to the present. The variation has often been great, so that today's phenomenon looks little like its antecedent, though caused by it, two or three or four thousand years ago, while there are also many differentiations in separate localities. Yet there must be something which in each successive periodic reincarnation of the civilization has caused the new existence of the civilization, something which in terms of the Buddhist doctrinal analogy corresponds to consciousness. To identify that something, assuming that it really is present, is the problem which I suggest deserves our attention. Its identification would contribute to our understanding of the process of Indian civilization, its past and its present, and give some hint, however slight or vague, of its future. The problem is essentially akin to that which Robert Redfield investigated in terms of the Great Tradition and the Little Tradition, or M. N. Srinivas treated under the heading of Sanskritization, or Milton Singer has recently been exploring as the relation between Text and Context. I hasten to say that I do not claim to have identified the vitalizing element, but I do wish to make a few remarks on the problem and shall be satisfied if I can help to define it more fully, even though I cannot achieve its solution.

The basic material for studying this problem is the mass of data available to us concerning the nature and development of civilization in India, the totality of items which reappear in altered form in the sequence of periods. Scholars have been assembling, synthesizing, and analyzing such material since the time of Christian Lassen, who published the first edition of his *Indische Alterthumskunde* in 1847. Other treatments have been L. D. Barnett's *Antiquities of India* in 1914, A. A. Macdonell's *India's Past* in 1927, L. Renou and J. Filliozat's

L'Inde Classique in 1947/1953. The most recent is A. L. Basham's *The Wonder that Was India,* which appeared in 1954. Such works easily establish the wide range of fields in which the continuity exists, the many aspects of life in which it is found.

These works and the specific researches on which they are based show us as well the great length of the continuity. There are, for example, certain items which appear throughout the entire 4,500 years of Indian civilization from the period of the Harappa culture in Western India in the third millennium B.C. to the present. Phallic worship is one of them; the use of the swastika symbol is another. A stylistic tradition in sculpture is still another, as Stella Kramrisch has pointed out. Though we have no interpretable data for ascertaining religious dogmas in the Harappa period, we see items in that culture which seem to indicate beliefs or practices similar to some now current. The pipal tree appears to have been honored or valued by the Harappa people; it is sacred today. The Harappans depicted on their seal-amulets the bull and the tiger, both of which have religious connotations today. They portray a wide variety of hybrid animals; similar animal hybridization continues in Hindu religious art. They presumably honored, perhaps worshipped, a three-faced anthropomorphic being whom they show seated in a yoga posture and surrounded by animals, recalling the god Shiva's aspect as the meditative ascetic deity and another of his aspects as Paśupati, "Lord of Animals." Unfortunately, we know nothing of the Harappa people's social structure and political organization, nor their language, nor their thought, and this, too, in spite of the fact that they left a script.

At a later period, when the Aryans had arrived in India and were producing the Vedic collections, in the second half of the second millennium B.C., roughly between 1500 and 1000, we see other cultural items that have had a series of metamorphoses in the interval down to the present. The high value set upon the cow is one, which by the beginning of the Christian era had led to the doctrine of the cow's sanctity or inviolability. The joint family system seems to have existed in the time of the Rig Veda; it is still the typical Hindu pattern. A special view of truth appears in the Rig Veda also, where it is invested with a kind of magic power that should probably be considered the starting point of many later conceptions of the power of truth, down to Gandhi's mystical theory about *satyāgraha.* The recorded history of speculative thought in India begins in the Rig Veda. Its start seems to have been the myth of the god Indra who slays the demon Vṛtra, releases the cosmic waters which were pregnant with the sun, and thus sets the stage for creation of the cosmos and the establishment of order in it. Out of this cosmological myth philosophy seems to have grown, with its subsequent manifold developments. The language of the Rig Veda, which is the earliest form of Sanskrit, served, as it developed into Classical Sanskrit, Pali, and the Prakrits, as the dominant vehicle of thought and culture in India until English superseded it in the nineteenth century, along with the body of western thought which it introduced. Even so Sanskrit is still remarkably alive and significant to Hindus.

A half a millennium after the Vedic period, Jainism and Buddhism put organized ascetism on a widely respected popular basis, where it still stands. These two faiths also promoted Ahinsa (*ahiṃsā*), "noninjury of living creatures," which remains to the present the most important ethical principle of Hinduism. They also accepted the joint doctrine of *karma* and rebirth, retribution for one's deeds in future existences, a doctrine already appearing in late Vedic thought, and popularized it until it was accepted as an axiom, and it continues to be so accepted in modern Hindu India.

At about the beginning of the Christian era, the social institution of caste, the rationalization of which was foreshadowed in Vedic literature as early as in the Puruṣa-sūkta of the Rig Veda (10.90), had been developed and was firmly established. With two millennia of development it is still the basic feature of Hindu social structure.

It would be possible to compile a catalogue of many hundreds of cultural items appearing in ancient Indian civilization which are then reborn or at least reappear in constantly changing fashion in succeeding periods during centuries, even millennia. Such a catalogue doubtless would not answer the question of what has given Indian civilization its special character and vitality, the element corresponding to the "consciousness" of Buddhist thought, without which new existences would not come into being, existences which, though new, are yet dependent upon preceding existences. Nor is that element likely to be identified even if we could classify the details of Indian civilization into categories by ethnic source, that is determine which were developed by Indo-Aryans, or by Dravidians, or by some other ethnic group, hoping in this way to identify a given people as the author of characteristic Indian civilization.

When I have asked Indians their thoughts on the question of a vitalizing element in Indian civilization, I have always had the answer that such an element certainly exists, but I have found difference of opinion as to what that element is. As simple an answer as I have ever received is that it is a special feeling for the sanctity of water. Such a feeling can be deduced from the elaborate bathing and drainage systems of town planning and architecture in the Harappa culture, the reverence for the Cosmic Waters in the Rig Veda, the use of ceremonial ablution in Hinduism, the veneration of streams and springs, and other lesser religious practices or taboos associated with water.

Oftener than any other the answer is that the determining element is the Indian concern with religio-philosophical investigation and its application to life. This is the search for metaphysical truth, the nature of the cosmos, of god, of the human soul, and of the Absolute and man's relation to it. The answer is in line with the common Indian view today that India throughout its history, down to and including the present, has been engrossed in the quest for the spiritual—in contrast with the West, which is considered to be preoccupied with "materialism." Aside from this bit of cultural chauvinism there is support for the general idea of India's especially intensive interest in religio-philosophic activity in the long history of speculative thought and religious teaching, so voluminously recorded in Indian literature from its beginnings in the Rig Veda, its blossoming in the Upanishads and in the Jain and Buddhist scriptures, and its wide ramification and varying development thereafter until our own day, witness Gandhi and Vinoba Bhave as contemporary illustrations; others could be named.

Some Indians, on being pressed further, have reduced their stress on this facet of Indian civilization and instead have placed it on the prevalence of tolerance, and pointed to the wide, often contradictory, yet tolerated, variation in Hinduism of intellectual dogma, and the accompanying latitudinarianism in views of human behavior. All these variations are accorded status in orthodox Hinduism.

This latter answer, or at least such a type of answer, seems to me to advance our investigation, but not to satisfy it. It carries us beyond material productions in the arts, literature, and sciences; beyond skills, customs, political institutions, social institutions, social change and development, varying norms, and thought forms; into the field of values and attitudes; and thus to the basis of behavior patterns.

Possibly we can take another step forward by looking at one of the values of Hinduism more closely. I am thinking of duty, and the unusual stress put upon correct action. Again, we can say nothing about this in the Harappa culture, but we can see it in the Rig Veda and still more markedly in the ritual worship described in the Yajur Veda and the Brāhmaṇas. In this ritual every detail must be perfect, and the priests are a highly trained fraternity with specialized duties painstakingly learned and performed with the finest exactitude. The doctrine of rebirth and *karma,* the most characteristic of all Indian religious teachings, employs this notion to its fullest. Every person's slightest action is a determinant of his future state, and the literature in thousands of passages points out in minute detail the correspondence between deed and result. In caste practice, behavior is the primary consideration; it must always accord with prescription, not only with respect to important matters such as marriage selection and birth and death ceremonies, but also with respect to such small ones as eating, speaking to or approaching others, or even the style of tonsure. Behavior far outweighs dogma in Hinduism, which may vary widely even for members of the same caste without objection from one's fellows. But not so with action! Infringement there results in penalty, which may extend to expulsion from the caste, social death.

Correct or right behavior is viewed as a personal responsibility or duty with a most significant meaning to Hindus, Buddhists, and Jains. Particular application of the idea of duty appears as early as in the Rig Veda. There it starts with the notion that our cosmos contains two opposing forces: that of ordered operation, progress, and harmonious cooperation of the parts; and that of disorder, chaos, destruction. The universe in which we live is held to operate under a code or set of principles to keep it going, and this code, this body of cosmic truth or order, has the name *satya* or *ṛta*. But disorder, anti-order, known as *anṛta,* is ever beating at our universe, tending to disrupt or destroy it. To keep our universe operating smoothly, every being in it has a function. Gods have their specific functions; human beings have their functions. No two gods have the same function, and human beings' functions also differ. Each god and each human must assiduously devote himself to his function. If he fails in performing it, to that extent the operation of the universe is impaired. The word for this individual function is *vrata* (RV 9.112), and so important is the concept that in post-Vedic times the word comes to mean a solemn, religious vow, to be undertaken with great seriousness and observed with unflagging zeal.

Human duty is differentiated in the Rig Veda for the four great classes of society: the Brahman (*brāhmaṇa*) or priest; the Rājanya or Kshatriya (*kṣatriya*), the temporal ruler or warrior; the Vaishya (*vaiśya*) or commoner, peasant and artisan; and the Shudra (*śūdra*) or slave. The Brāhmaṇa celebrates the ritual, first performed at the time of creation by the gods, and this ritual gives the gods the help they need to counteract the destructive force of evil. The Kṣatriya patronizes the sacrifice and protects it from harm. The Vaiśya produces the economic means needed by the ruler and the Brāhmaṣa. The Śūdra does menial service for the others in their activities. In RV 10.90, creation is described figuratively as the primordial sacrifice by the gods of a being called Purusha (*puruṣa*), "male," a symbolic representation of all the materials needed to produce the universe. As he is dismembered, the parts of his body become the parts of the universe. There it is said that "the Brāhamaṇa was Puruṣa's mouth, the Rājanya was made into his arms; as for his thighs, that was what the Vaiśya became; from his feet the Śūdra was born." The symbolism is obvious.

After the caste system with its practice of endogamy and its ideas of pollution emerged by the beginning of the Christian era or earlier, it was artificially encased by orthodox Hindu priestly thought into the four-class system of Vedic society. Manu, author of the great and well-known legal text, ascribes the multiplicity of castes to mixture of the four original social groups, an evil practice in his opinion. Nevertheless, Hinduism eventually applied to the whole caste system the rationalizing theory that each caste has a specific function in the universe which it is duty bound to perform. Each individual member of a caste has as his personal duty that of fulfilling the function of his caste; if he avoids it, he commits sin.

Though this kind of rationalization is both bad anthropology and bad history, not to speak of dubious metaphysics, it has nevertheless had deep influence and led to important consequences, especially when it became associated with the doctrine of *karma* and rebirth. First, as we have already noticed, reward for doing one's duty or punishment for failure to do it were held to be experienced in rebirth and to determine the conditions of rebirth. Second, one's present caste status was considered to be the consequence of deeds done in previous existences. Birth in a high caste was a reward, birth in a low caste a punishment. Furthermore, the intellectual and spiritual, sometimes even the moral, endowments of a person at birth were regarded as a concomitant of his caste status. Hence a low caste person was expected to have a less sophisticated view of god, society, life, and morality than a high caste person. That was part of his general lowly estate. He must therefore not be expected to comprehend what the high caste person was equipped to comprehend. So, too, standards of behavior were viewed as different. Normal conduct for a low caste man might be sin for a Brahman. All this was understood to be in accord with cosmic law. It constituted an acceptance of relativity concerning human capacity and human behavior that is the basis of the Hindu tolerance mentioned above. There was no such thing as a single universal standard of duty. Not all people were or could rationally be expected to comprehend the same ideas or to live by the same codes. Each caste could quite legitimately frame its own rules for fulfilling its caste function—within limits, of course—so long as the observance of them did not interfere with another caste in the fulfilling of its function and the observance of its rules. This was the adjustment that made it possible for contradictory doctrines and conflicting codes to dwell side by side in peaceful coexistence. Divergency of duty was expected, accepted, and legitimized on what might seem to others to be a scale of astounding amplitude.

Other large or basic values of Indian civilization might be cited for examination, such as truth and Ahinsa, which have already been mentioned, or the attitude toward law as something not made by man, not even by the king—the Bṛhadāraṇyaka Upanishad (1.4.14) says law is "king over the king"—not invented by kings or by the gods or even by God, but existing before and independently of them all. Should we think that any such value or a whole set of values has constituted the feature giving Indian civilization its vitality throughout history? I repeat that I should not want to make a positive asseveration that it has, but I think the possibility may at least be worthy of consideration, and, in that case, the identification, description, and application of these values deserve deep study.

In viewing Indian civilization I am reminded of the banyan tree, a fig tree, in Sanskrit called *nyagrodha,* a word which means "the down-grower." Though this tree begins life with a single trunk rising from a minute seed, its wide-spreading branches send down air roots, some of which themselves reach the ground, penetrate it, and become secondary trunks, occasionally to rival in size the first trunk. Thus the tree may come to shade an acre or more of ground. One can imagine a banyan tree of such age and such coverage that it may have a number of secondary trunks capable of being confused at first glance with the primary trunk. Such, it seems to me, has been the history of Indian civilization. It arose from roots in the subsurface culture of India, the material of Redfield's Little Tradition or Singer's Contextual. It grew up and spread out into the Great Tradition and the Textual. As it grew it sent out branches, and these sent down air roots, some of which returned into the soil and so became the means of communication between subsurface roots and above-ground branches. This was always a two-way communication, though a selective one with respect to the items communicated, implementing a constant process of mutual feed and feedback, of reciprocal input and output.

But the animating principle of the Nyagrodha is not easy to discern. There is a passage in the Chāndogya Upanishad (6.12) touching on that point. The setting is that of Śvetaketu Āruṇeya being instructed by his father Uddālaka, after Śvetaketu has come back from his twelve-year course of study, conceited and proud, thinking that he had mastered all knowledge. Uddālaka sets out to teach him something he has not learned, namely, how to know the one thing that gives knowledge of all other things. This is, it happens, the *ātman* (Soul), which permeates all beings, is uniform, invariable, and indestructible. He teaches partly by parable, and one of the parables concerns the Nyagrodha fig tree, the banyan. Uddālaka speaks to his son:

"Bring hither a fig from there." "Here it is, sir." "Split it." "It is split, sir." "What do you see there?" "These rather fine seeds, sir." "Please split one of these." "It is split, sir." "What do you see there?" "Nothing at all, sir." Then Uddālaka said to him, "Verily, my dear, the finest essence which you do not perceive—verily, my dear, from that finest essence this great *nyagrodha* tree thus arises." And he concludes by saying that that essence is the essence of the whole world, of Śvetaketu himself; that it *is* Śvetaketu.

Perhaps any efforts of ours to find the seed that has been the vitalizing essence of Indian civilization, its principle of consciousness, to use the Buddhist doctrinal analogy, may be as futile as Śvetaketu's effort to see the essence of the banyan tree. Such a failure might still not convince an inquirer that a vitalizing element was not there, nor prevent the curious from seeking for it. Śvetaketu, of course, had only his eyes with which to look.

1.
The Search for the Real

In one of the early Upanishads (BAU 1.3.28) the patron of a sacrifice is admonished to mutter the following prayer:

> From the Unreal lead me to the Real!
> From Darkness lead me to Light!
> From Death lead me to Immortality!

The text then goes on to explain that the Unreal, Darkness, and Death are all the same, and the Real, Light, and Immortality are also the same. The whole prayer then, the text says, means, "Lead me from Death to Immortality!"

The words used in this prayer at once echo early Rigvedic man's deepest fears and hopes, use the terminology of India's earliest recorded metaphysical speculations, and forecast the goal in later times of her most devoted seekers of knowledge and salvation. They voice the ideal today of those thinkers following the ancient tradition who seek to penetrate the cosmic mystery and search for a way out for man from his predicament before it.

Yet the meaning of the terms Unreal (*asat*) and Real (*sat*), Darkness (*tamas*) and Light (*jyoti*), Death (*mṛtyu*) and Immortality (*amṛta*), and specific significance of these concepts, has not remained constant. Only the desire to identify and know the Real has continued unaltered, a consistent value in India's intellectual history. The aim has been a homogeneous, continuous white warp on which has been woven a varicolored, many-patterned, ever-changing, always new sequence of metaphysical speculation and has given the parts a relationship to one another. The purpose of this lecture is to describe the sequence of some thousand years of the pattern woven on that underlying warp. We may start with the earliest recorded theorizing, a half a millennium or so before the time of the Upanishadic text in which the prayer appears.

In India's oldest book, the Rig Veda, generally thought to have been finally compiled by 1000 B.C., there seems to be an accepted and unargued view of the constitution of our universe. Let me describe it briefly: [1] Rigvedic man considered the universe to consist of two parts, placed one above the other. The upper part, a hemisphere, was that in which men and the gods live, and it consisted of the earth's broad surface, the vault of the sky above it, and the atmosphere between the two. This upper part of the universe he called the Sat, which means, "the Existent, the Real." The lower part, reached from the earth by a great chasm, was a place of horror, inhabited by demons. This he called the Asat, which means "the Anti-Sat, the Nonexistent, the Unreal." The creatures of the two parts were in a natural state of enmity with each other, and the two regions themselves were antithetical. In the Sat were light, warmth, moisture—requisites for life—and these and all the phenomena of nature concerned with their appearance, operation, and use were subject to a body of universal cosmic law or truth called the Ṛta. To make the Sat function perfectly, that is, according to the Ṛta, man had a duty to perform, which was double in character. One part was to patronize the Vedic sacrifice, make the proper ritual offerings to the gods. The other part was to fulfill his personal function (*vrata*) in the world. When he fulfilled this double duty, he was an observer of the Ṛta (*ṛtavan*). The result for him, whether man or god, was life, growth, prosperity.

In the Asat the essentials for life and growth were lacking. There was no sun and no moisture. There were instead cold, darkness, drought, and the place was without the Ṛta (*anṛta*), that is, without cosmic truth and law, being a fearful chaos. Decay and death marked it. The creatures of the Asat, who were demons, would emerge into the Sat by way of the chasm that connected them, especially in the dark of the night, which for Vedic man was a time of dread, as it still is to this day for the more simple-minded folk in India who fear the demons and spirits (*bhūt*) then on the prowl. When the demons of the Asat came up into the Sat, their purpose was to catch and destroy unwary men. And when a man died and was seeking his way up to the heaven of the blessed at the top of the universe, pursuing the path long ago discovered by Yama, the first man, they hovered beside it to waylay him. He needed the protection of Yama's two dogs that guard the path, and this he got provided he had lived righteously, that is, according to the Ṛta, had fulfilled his personal duty, had patronized the sacrifice, made the prescribed offerings, bestowed generous fees upon the priests who officiated, and honored the gods. If he had not, he got no protection from Yama's dogs, and the demons met no interference but seized and destroyed him. The Asat and its inhabitants constitute the Rigvedic conception nearest the Western notion of Hell and the Devil or devils.

The prayer which I cited at the beginning of this address appears in an Upanishad which must be at least three or four centuries later than the final compilation of the Rig Veda, while the Rig Veda itself was many centuries in growth, how many centuries we cannot say but presumably between two and five. The prayer, however, would have been appropriate at any time during the Rigvedic period from the beginning on. "From the Unreal (*asat*) lead me to the Real (*sat*)." The Unreal and the Real, the *asat* and the *sat*, as we have just described them, would have had a very concrete meaning to Rigvedic man. Similarly, the words, "From Darkness lead me to Light," had a definite concrete significance, being a prayer to lead one from the darkness of the Asat to the light of the Sat, and the words, "From Death lead me to Immortality," would have been a prayer to be saved from destruction by the demons of the Asat and instead to reach the joyous immortality of Yama's heaven at the top of the Sat.

But in spite of the fact that the prayer would have been just as applicable in the earliest Rigvedic times as in the Upanishadic period, five hundred to perhaps a thousand years later, the conceptions of the Real and the Unreal, the true and the false, were vastly different in the Upanishad and the Rig Veda. Beliefs concerning the cosmos and the nature of man had changed, and the process of change had begun in the Rig Veda itself. We can trace the successive steps in the development of cosmogonic speculation, which in India as in Greece was the beginning of philosophy, and this we should now do. We shall then be prepared to consider further speculative developments in the Upanishads.

The first Indian ideas about the origin of the Sat and the Asat, the hemispheres of Rigvedic man's universe, are embedded in the myth of the hero god Indra and his mortal battle with Vṛtra, the chief of the demons. This is the most important myth of the Rig Veda, the one most often recounted or alluded to, and it receives the most attention in the Rigvedic sacrifice and has the most influence in shaping its ritual. The myth starts with conditions before creation. At that time there was no Sat or Asat, no separation of the Real from the Unreal. Nor was there the Ṛta, the body of cosmic law or truth governing the Real, the Sat. Neither were there men in existence. There were, however, beings called Asura, living sentient entities possessed of will and great power. These were of two sorts. One, the myth called Aditya; the name means "being who is devoted to release, expansion, growth, development." The Ādityas, we might say, were liberals, progressives. The other was called Dānava; the name means "being who is devoted to bondage or restraint or non-expansion, committed to inertia." We might call a Dānava a conservative, a reactionary, one opposed to change or development. The chief Dānava was Vṛtra, whose name means "covering, lid, enclosure." The chief of the Ādityas was Varuṇa, whose name is of uncertain origin. The names of the figures appearing in the myth, as far as we understand them, show that those figures are personifications of abstractions.

With respect to the creation of an ordered universe, the Ādityas were positive, benevolent; hence they are presented as beings standing for good. The Dānavas were negative toward creation and order, malevolent, beings of evil. The Ādityas and the Dānavas were in a state of war, which had reached a stalemate or was going badly for the Ādityas. But by some means the Ādityas succeeded in getting a champion born, the god Indra, probably the son of Mother Earth and Father Sky. The name Indra has defied any convincing etymology, but he has various epithets which seem to indicate that he personifies the physical power lying in nature, especially that in the realm where he lives and operates, which is the atmosphere; his might is most potently and dramatically exhibited in the storm.

When the Ādityas, immediately after Indra was born, sought his aid, he first exacted a promise that he should be the supreme king. Next he took three enormous draughts of a powerful and mysterious drink called *soma,* brought to him by some marvelous means, which aroused his fighting fury, gave him overpowering strength, and caused him to swell to enormous and terrifying size so that he permanently drove apart Heaven and Earth, which until then had been united, while he himself now filled the intervening space. Then armed with a mighty weapon called *vajra,* fashioned for him by Tvashtri (*tvaṣṭṛ*), the artificer of the gods, and generally considered to be the lightning, he engaged in battle with Vṛtra. After a fierce fight he was finally victorious, slaying Vṛtra or, as the texts sometimes put it, bursting his belly.

The Ādityas' specific war aims then become apparent. For when Indra slew Vṛtra, there flowed out from confinement in the cave which he had been covering or out of his burst belly the seven cosmic waters or rivers, and these waters astonishingly were pregnant, and their single joint embryo was the sun. Thus the light and heat of the sun and the moisture of the cosmic waters, which were all needed to sustain life, were at hand, and creation and organization of the universe could take place. The earth was spread out and stabilized. The sky was pegged in place at the corners of the earth. The Ṛta (cosmic truth or law) was proclaimed, and the various Ādityas were assigned their functions under it, with Varuṇa, their chief, given special charge over its enforcement. The waters became the heavenly ocean, from which they descend to the earth; the sun was set on its course, and Indra was sole emperor (*eka samrāṭ*) over all. In due time man came into existence on earth, where he performs the sacrifice which gives nourishment to the gods and supports the Ṛta. Evil, however, was not extinguished. Though Vṛtra had been slain, the demons still had their place in the Asat, where they lived and bred, and the war between the demons and the gods has continued ever since, with man in the middle. Man in general has been allied to the gods, as is to his interest, but there have always been human misfits, foolish creatures misguided enough to practice witchcraft and sorcery in cooperation with the demons, a misalliance and blunder that inevitably leads those men to destruction.

This myth was doubtless viewed literally by the generality of Rigvedic men, but the intellectually more sophisticated must have taken it as an allegory. The etymological meanings of the names Āditya, Dānava, Vṛtra, would seem to indicate as much. As an allegory, the myth would have dealt with the opposition between the impersonal forces of conservatism, inertia, stagnation on the one side and on the other those of liberalism, progress, change, evolution, with the latter triumphing through the dynamism inherent in nature. This last produced stability in the universe by a multitude of accommodations between physical forces, constituting the code of natural law known as the Ṛta. But the tendency toward inertia is ever present in our world, and man must constantly and positively nurture progress. Each day the battle must be renewed, for this is the price of a harmoniously operating cosmic machine.

The process of supplanting the Indra-Vṛtra myth as a theory of creation had started before the compilation of the Rig Veda was complete. There were theistically inclined hymn composers who seem to have considered Indra too anthropomorphic a creator to be acceptable.

There were ritualists who were increasingly insisting that creation was a product of a properly performed sacrifice. And there were early metaphysicians who were evolving new mechanistic theories of creation.

Direct skepticism about Indra is shown in various passages, for example (RV 8.100.3): "Bring lovely praise to Indra, vying with one another, truthful praise, if he himself be true—even though one or the other says, Indra is not! Who ever saw him? Who is he that we should praise him?" An explicit repudiation of Indra appears in a theistically motivated hymn dedicated to the god Ka, whose name is merely the interrogative pronoun "Who." In stanza after stanza the hymn mentions some great deed or some exalted distinction, and then asks who the god is to whom we should offer oblation for having performed that deed or won that distinction. These deeds and distinctions, it happens, are ones that are elsewhere regularly ascribed to Indra: the making firm of earth and sky; rulership over the gods; the bestowing of victory upon one of two rival armies; the release of the waters; the inauguration of the sacrifice; the status of sole, that is, supreme god. In the final stanza the god to be worshipped for all these accomplishments and attainments is named. But though we and the ordinary Rigvedic man would expect the name to be that of Indra, it is not, and was presumably meant to come as a surprise. For the name of the god is Prajāpati, which means "Lord of Creatures," and he is an obvious heiratic invention, a designation of an unknown quantity like the *x* which is the answer to an algebraic equation. The figure of Prajāpati, once it was invented in Rigvedic times, continues long afterwards and even attains a tenuous jejune kind of anthropomorphism, but it never acquires much personality, standing in marked contrast to the blustering, roaring, *soma*-drinking, bolt-wielding, battle-loving, joyously dancing, triumph-celebrating, impetuously generous Indra, whom he has here superseded.

Another theistic figure hypothesized in place of Indra is Viśvakarman. The name means "Maker of All," and in one passage it is actually used as an epithet of Indra (RV 8.98.2), but there are two entire hymns (RV 10.81 and 82) in which Viśvakarman is an independent deity, a superdeity like Prajāpati, but unlike Prajāpati in the hymn we mentioned above, not spoken of in terms drawn from Indra's mythology. In the two hymns addressed to Viśvakarman he is set above the older gods of the Rig Veda, and conceived in loftier, more clearly monotheistic terms than any of them, including Indra. As "our father" he instituted, or taught the sages how to institute, the sacrifice, the holy ceremony which resulted in creation. In this way he produced heaven and earth, though where he took his stand in doing so and what materials he used are questions which the hymn poses for answer. He is supreme, and where he is there the righteous dead enjoy the fruit of the sacrificial offerings they have made. He seems to have created the gods, for one of the hymns says he gave them their names, which should mean that when he pronounced their names they came into existence (RV 10.82.3; cf. RV 10.71.1). When the gods, after being brought into existence, assembled to celebrate the sacrifice, the waters set down the primeval germ or embryo, which was beyond, that is, above, heaven and earth, beyond the gods and the demons, and the gods offered it in the sacrificial fire. This germ contained all the insentient material of the universe, and this the gods organized when Viśvakarman taught them the sacrificial ritual. In the Viśvakarman hymns the epistemological question is raised; it had not been broached in the Indra-Vṛtra myth. Knowledge, one of the hymns says, comes from

Viśvakarman; all creatures go to him for it (RH 10.82.3). But nowadays the chanters of hymns (meaning priests) do not know who created all things (RV 10.82.7); for knowledge a man of mystic insight must inquire with his own mind, that is, resort to introspection (RV 10.81.4). Through this means he can learn the answers to the questions posed above, namely, what material Viśvakarman used and where he took his stand when he fashioned heaven and earth.

Though Prajāpati and Viśvakarman are conceived as superdeities responsible for the existence of gods and men and the organization of the material substance of the universe, and though the epistemological question has been raised in one of the Viśvakarman hymns, the hymns addressed to those two figures do not deal with the origin itself of the insentient material of which the universe is composed. That point, however, is considered in connection with the god Brahmaṇaspati. This god, who is also known as Bṛhaspati, is another late hieratic invention, and his name, like the names Prajāpati and Viśvakarman, is more an epithet or title than a genuine proper name. Brahmaṇaspati means, "lord of the holy or mystic power called *brahman*," which the Vedas represent as permeating the universe, and Bṛhaspati means "lord of the holy prayer or utterance or devotion (*bṛh*)" that evokes the *brahman* and sets it in operation. Through the concept of Brahmaṇaspati or Bṛhaspati a displacement of Indra takes place, which is less direct than that through Prajāpati or Viśvakarman. Brahmaṇaspati and Indra are represented in several hymns as cooperating to perform some of the greatest of the deeds elsewhere usually ascribed to Indra alone: winning the light for the universe, spreading out the earth, and others. The hieratic point of view leading to the creation of Brahmaṇaspati seems to be that the great deeds which Indra was said to have performed could not have been performed through mere physical might, but were really made possible metaphysically through the mystic power in the universe which was put into application through the sacrifice. Hence the two deities are viewed as cooperating (RV 2.24, 10.67). The next step was to ascribe the action to Brahmaṇaspati alone with Indra ignored (RV 10.68). Then comes the ascription of all creation to Brahmaṇaspati, and in terms that transcend the Indra-Vṛtra range of achievement (RV 10.72).

Brahmaṇaspati, we are told (RV 10.72), "blew up" the material of the universe, like a smith at his forge. First, says the hymn, he generated the Sat from the Asat. The Asat, unordered chaos, is here also called Uttānapad, "she with legs outspread [in parturition]." Thus we have the old notion that the ordered universe was born out of the unordered chaos. From the Sat, in turn, were produced the directions. Parallel to the origin of the material substance of the universe was the origin of animate, sentient beings. These came from Dakṣa—the name means essentially male potentiality—and Aditi, who is female productive or creative power. Each of this pair, the hymn says, was produced from the other, which seems to be a way of saying that the two are interdependent. Where they came from is not otherwise stated. Possibly we are to understand that Brahmaṇaspati created them, or possibly they were thought to be self-existent forces which acted upon, or in concert with, each other. From Aditi were born the seven Ādityas, who took their place in the tumultuous chaos and with linked hands stirred up the dust as though dancing. Thus they produced the worlds and found the sun, another Āditya, who was their own youngest brother, the eighth son of Aditi. The seven elder Ādityas were immortal, but Aditi produced her eighth son, as the hymn says, "to be born and then to die again." Thus mortality came into the universe. In this hymn, as in the Viś-vakarman hymns, the epistemological question is raised, and again the answer is that knowledge of "the origins of the gods" comes in this later age to the one who can see those origins when the hymns are being recited. This means that the seer is to practise introspection under the mystic influence of the chants of the sacrifice.

The significance of the concept of Brahmaṇaspati or Bṛhaspati is possibly that late in the Rigvedic period the power of the ritual had come to be considered greater than that of the gods whom the priests invoked with the aid of ritual. It was greater even than the power of Indra. Hence Indra's great feat could exist only through the use of the sacrifice and its mystical or magic power, which was then deified as Brahmaṇaspati or Bṛhaspati.

The exaltation of the power of the sacrifice to effect creation is developed with still greater specificity in the hymn of Puruṣa (RV 10.90). Puruṣa means "male, man," and in the hymn he is the sacrificial victim. Puruṣa, the hymn makes clear, contains within himself all the raw material of the cosmos and more besides but still in an unordered state. It includes not only the inanimate world but all mortal creatures and the immortal beings as well. Two-thirds of the hymn is an account of the sacrifice and an enumeration of its constituents. Among the latter are the orders of society—the Brāhmaṇa (priest, spiritual aristocracy) as the mouth of the sacrifice, the Rājanya (warrior, ruler, secular aristocracy) as its arms, the Vaiśya (merchant, artisan, commons) as its thighs. The hymns mention all that was produced from Puruṣa, including the Śūdras (serfs) and the animals; earth, sky, and the atmosphere; the moon and the sun; also the sacred hymns, the chants, the metres, and the prose formulae used in the sacrifice; and even the gods Indra, Agni (the ancient god of the sacrifice), and Vāyu (god of the wind). Who the gods were who performed the sacrifice is not clear since they are not specified in the hymn, but it is a fair guess that they were the Ādityas. The point of view of the hymn is purely hieratic, and the hymn is the Rig Veda's most extreme magnification of the metaphysical potency, the ritualistic magic of the elaborate ceremony which the sacrifice had become by the time when the compilation of the Rig Veda was completed.

Because of the importance of the ritual in Rigvedic thinking, the holy Word came to be regarded as being in itself supremely efficacious. It is personified and deified as the feminine Vāc, which means "speech, sound, word," and she says of herself (RV 10.125) that her birthplace was in the waters, whence she spread out on all sides over the world and reached the sky, surpassing the universe. Though the hymns do not say so explicitly, she is described in terms which seem to indicate that she is conceived as the creative power that produced and shaped the cosmos.

In the various ideas that we have been considering there has been no statement or even implication that the universe originated in some single principle. There is no hint of monism; the hymns cited have merely each one tried to identify a more remote active agent than any previously indicated. Further, these hymns all state explicitly or else tacitly imply that there are two principles in the universe, two kinds of components. One is animate or psychical, involving the power of will and appearing in the gods or a god or an overgod or superdeity. The other is nonpsychical, inanimate, devoid of will; it is the material part of the universe, the object upon which the first acts as subject. But by the end of the Rigvedic period the monistic idea has appeared. It is possibly implied in several brief passages (such as RV 1.164.46), but it is explicitly developed in one remarkable hymn (RV 10.129). This is so important and so suggestive for post-Rigvedic speculation that we may profitably give it our special attention.

The hymn ignores the creative role of a demiurge or a superdeity or the sacrifice, simply bypassing them. Instead, it posits a single principle which it calls Tad Ekam. The two Vedic words are a neuter pronoun and a numeral, and they mean, "That One" or "the one thing." This, says the hymn, existed before the Asat and the Sat, before the gods or before their overseer in the highest heaven, that is, before any superdeity. It was self-existent, coming into being spontaneously. Once it had come into existence, it experienced desire (*kāma*), the first seed of mind. The implication seems to be that this desire stimulated production of the manifold constituents of our universe. The epistemological question gets an answer, too. We know about the beginning not through any line of transmission from the beginning itself, for even the gods are created beings and do not know the origins. Rather, the hymn says, the [seven primeval] sages discovered how it all came about by pious insight into their own hearts—that is, again, by introspection. Let us look at the whole hymn in translation:

RIG VEDA 10.129

1. There was not then either the Nonexistent (Asat) or the Existent (Sat). There was no sky nor heavenly vault beyond it. What covered all? Where? What was its protection? Was there a fathomless depth of the waters?
2. There was neither death nor immortality then. There was the sheen neither of day nor of night. That One breathed (came to life), though uninspired by breath, by its own potentiality. Besides it nothing existed.
3. There was darkness hidden by darkness at the beginning. This all was an unillumined flood. The

force (with power of evolution) which was hidden by a shell, That One, was born through the power of its own (creative incubating) heat.

4. In the beginning desire grew in That [One], which became the first seed of mind. The sages by their pious insight in their heart (i.e., by introspection) found the relation of the Existent with the Non-existent.
5. A line of demarcation was extended horizontally for them. What was below it, what was above it? There were seed-depositors, there were powers. There was potentiality here below, there was emanation above.
6. Who is there who knows, who here (*iha*) can tell whence was the origin, and whence this creation? The gods are this side of the creation. Who knows, then, whence it came into being?
7. This creation, whence it came into being, whether spontaneously or not—he who is its highest overseer in heaven, he surely knows, or perhaps he knows not.

This hymn is India's first unequivocal presentation of the monistic idea, which afterwards becomes so productive. The Vedic thinkers have advanced a long way from the Indra-Vṛtra myth in their search for the Real, though much more development is to come. There is still lacking in this hymn—or in any other Rigvedic hymn—explicit reference to soul or self (*ātman*), though some orthodox Brahmanical thinkers consider the idea implicit in it. The monistic principle, which here bears the name That One, is the Brahman, mentioned above as the mystic metaphysical power in the universe which can be evoked and activated by the potent prayer (*bṛh*), the forces incorporated in the names Brahmaṇaspati and Bṛhaspati. In this hymn that power has been redefined, transfigured, and is ready to become transcendental.

Two other efforts to isolate a single unifying principle

in the universe appear in the Atharva Veda, which as a whole is later than the Rig Veda. One of these specifies Time (*kāla*) as the all-inclusive single principle. Two hymns are devoted to it (AV 19.53 and 54). In Time, they proclaim, lie the worlds and the suns. By Time the universe was urged forth. Time is Brahman. In Time the waters exist. From Time arose Brahman, the sacred hymns, the prose formulae of the sacrifice. Time contains and conquers all, and still continues onward. The other newly advanced idea in the Atharva Veda is that of a Frame (*skambha*) containing within it all that constitutes the universe (AV 10.7 and 10.8).

Neither the idea of all-inclusive Time nor that of an all-encompassing Frame stands up later in competition with the idea of Tad Ekam, That One. Time as the all-container may have been held to deal with the temporal antinomy, but it ignores the antinomies of space and cause and effect. Similarly, the idea of the all-enveloping Frame may have been thought to account for the spatial antinomy, but it does not deal with the antinomies of time and cause and effect. The That One concept, in being viewed as satisfying the antinomy of cause and effect, was also probably felt to satisfy the other two antinomies as well. The Tad Ekam teaching, however, was not idealistic; it was a realistic monism, and as such it passed from the Rig Veda to the Upanishadic thinkers.

The development of Rigvedic speculative thought which we have been observing extended over a long period of time. The Indra-Vṛtra myth was known to the Indo-Aryans before their entry into India, for it is a variant of a myth that was common Indo-Iranian property. At the latest it must have come into India by 1200 B.C., and the date may have been as much as three or even more centuries earlier. The various speculative hymns we have cited are all regarded as "late," that is, they are thought to have been composed not much earlier than 1000 B.C., by which date the compilation of the Rig Veda is generally thought to have been completed. The period of time involved in the evolution we have been tracing, therefore, would have been at a minimum two hundred years, and very likely some centuries more than that.

The Upanishadic period was also long. Upanishadic ideas were presumably being discussed from about the time of the completion of the Rig Veda or shortly afterwards down through the period of composition of the principal Upanishads themselves, which it is usually thought continued to around 500 B.C. or perhaps even later. This means that the evolution of Upanishadic thought took place during a period of half a millennium if not longer.

The Upanishads are among the world's great intellectual creations. They do not teach a single philosophic system nor do they teach a number of systems, for they are not systematic in their method. They advance ideas in a tentative, experimental fashion, disagreeing with one another and exhibiting an ever-changing series of efforts to penetrate the mystery of the cosmos and man's relation to it. Fresh intellectual approaches are entertained with ready hospitality in the texts and old ideas are abandoned with no regrets. The texts are transmitted orally; hence they often use obvious mnemonic devices, such as repetition. But they also have an easy and informal literary style and employ narrative, parable, illustration, figures of speech, dialogue, Socratic questioning, poetry, all so skillfully and appositely that the didactic purpose never becomes oppressive, while instead they sustain the reader's—or hearer's—lively interest. The philosophic discourses of the sage Yājñavalkya with King Janaka or with his truth-seeking wife Maitreyī, the instruction which King Ajātaśatru gave to the learned Brahman Gārgya, the teaching which Uddālaka imparted to his son Śvetaketu as they sat beneath the banyan tree, above all the persistence with which the youthful Naciketas pressed the advantage he had accidentally acquired over the god Death to wring from him an answer to the question of what happens to a person after he dies—these would be classic passages in any literature.

It is not my purpose to give a full report on the history of Indian philosophy or even its early periods, nor to try to treat adequately the many different teachings of the Upanishads, nor even to give them as much attention as we have given to the beginning of speculative thought in the late Rig Veda. Rather, the purpose now will be only to point out major ideas advanced in the Upanishads and to mention a few others appearing later, so as to illustrate the ever-changing nature of Brahmanic-Hindu thought in the persistent search to find the Real and to turn the knowledge so won to some practical use.

The monistic view of the universe which the Rig Veda bequeathed to the Upanishads is the first of the great teachings in those works, and it is elaborated in text after text.[2] The Real is Brahman, and we may cite an illustrative passage: "This [universe] is that [sole principle], even the Real. He who knows that great wonderful thing as the first-born—namely, that Brahman is the Real—conquers these worlds. Would he be conquered who knows thus that great wonderful thing as the first-born—namely, that Brahman is the Real? [No!] for indeed Brahman is the Real" (BAU 5.4). The teaching of this passage is that Brahman is not merely the source of all or pervades all, but that Brahman actually is all. Or, in another passage: "Brahman, indeed, is this immortal: in front is Brahman, behind is Brahman, to right and to left, stretched forth below and above. Brahman, indeed, is this whole world, this widest extent" (Muṇḍ 2.2.11). This conception of Brahman as the first and only principle is based on a view of the phenomenal world as real. There is no hint yet of the doctrine that the phenomenal world is illusion.

Another pantheistic or monistic doctrine which appears in the ontology of the Upanishads is that the Real is the Ātman, the self or soul. This is conceived on the cosmic scale, and the cosmic self is understood to be of the same character as the individual's Self or Soul. It is not easy to find the root of such a doctrine in the Rig Veda, for that book says nothing about the Ātman, whether cosmic or individual. It has been suggested [3] that the Upanishadic doctrine may be related to the notion of the sacrifice of Puruṣa (male) as an act of creation. Whatever the truth may be about that Rigvedic hymn, the description of the cosmos in terms of the human body appears several times in the Upanishads and leads eventually to an identification of the cosmic macrocosm with the human microcosm. The teaching therefore follows that by knowing one's own self one comes to know the world all. On this assumption the cosmic epistemological question is again explicitly answered by introspection. "Ātman alone," says a passage (CU 7.25.2) "is this whole world!"

By an application of the principle that things equal to the same thing are equal to one another, it was a logical conclusion that the individual Self as equivalent to the world Self should also be taken as equivalent to the Brahman which is the essence of the phenomenal world. The resulting position was that the Brahman and the individual Ātman were identical. To restate the doctrine: the Real is unitary; it is the universal essence or Self, and it is also the individual Self. The terms Brahman and Ātman are accordingly treated as interchangeable (Muṇḍ 2.2.5). This leads to such statements as *ahaṃ brahmāsmi,* "I am Brahman" (BAU 1.4.10), and whoever knows this of himself becomes this all; even the gods cannot prevent him, for he becomes their Self (*ātman,* BAU 1.4.10). Or it produces the great instruction which Uddālaka gave to his son Śvetaketu, who had been a student of holy lore for twelve years and had mastered the hymns and explanations of the Vedas and knew the intricacies of ritual but had not learned the most fundamental thing and had to be taught it by his father. This was the teaching "whereby what has not been heard of becomes heard of, what has not been thought of becomes thought of, what has not been understood becomes understood." It is a teaching through which "by one piece of clay everything made of clay may be known—the modification is merely a verbal distinction, a name; the reality is just 'clay!' " Just so "by one copper ornament everything made of copper may be known . . . by one nail-scissors everything made of iron may be known . . ." (CU 6.1.6). In a series of parables and illustrations (CU 6.9–16) Uddālaka drives home the point and at the end of each pronounces: "That which is the finest essence—this whole world has that as its soul. That is Reality. That is Ātman. That art thou, Śvetaketu." The last words are the famous phrase *tat tvam asi śvetaketo.*

The Soul or Self, Ātman, however, is indescribable, unknowable except by itself. It cannot be comprehended through sensory experience. "It is not this, it is not that. It is unseizable, for it cannot be seized. It is indestructible, for it cannot be destroyed. It is unattached, for it does not attach itself. It is unbound. It does not tremble. It is not injured" (BAU 4.2.4). The Ātman is pure subject. It can see, smell, taste, speak, hear, think, touch, know—that is, it has these capabilities. But it does not see, smell, taste, speak to, hear, think of, touch, know anything, because it is the sole reality, unaccompanied by a second thing which it might see, smell, taste, etc. (BAU 4.3.23–31). It can experience only itself, for in the absolute sense there is nothing else for it to experience. It is pure consciousness, with no second thing to be conscious of. This is pure idealism. For the Ātman to realize itself is the highest bliss. That person who has realized his soul, who has realized Brahman, for whom Brahman has become his world—that person is single, clear, transparent like pure water, without duality. To reach that state is man's highest path. This is his highest achievement. This is his highest world. This is his highest bliss. On a part of just this bliss other creatures have their living (BAU 4.3.32). In post-Upanishadic times that state is characterized as *saccidānanda* "Reality, Consciousness, Bliss," all in their pure state, not capable of being described.

In many places in the Upanishads this supreme state is related to, yet made to transcend, human experience, through reference to the three states of consciousness. The first of these states is that of waking—our normal living state. The second is that of dreaming sleep (*svapna*). The third is deep, dreamless sleep (*suṣupti*). In this last the soul has realized itself, and enjoys bliss beyond any description, not capable of apprehension by our senses or of being reported about through the use of our sense organs. At death, this state is achieved permanently by one who is released, one who, a text says, does not desire, who is without desire, who is freed from desire, whose desire is satisfied, whose desire is the Soul. Being very Brahman, he goes to Brahman (BAU 4.4.6). But the man who has not rid himself of desire, who is not freed from desire, is reborn in some other form, and the form is determined for him by his conduct in this life: the doer of good fares well, the doer of evil fares ill (BAU 4.4.3–6). Late in the Upanishadic period that state which cannot be described except as one of existence, pure consciousness, and bliss is denominated simply as the "fourth" state (*caturtha, turīya, turya*—Māṇḍ 5; Maitri 6.19, 7.11.7).

Here is a goal, the highest toward which one may strive. But how can one reach it? The old Vedic sacrifice will not suffice. Neither will worship avail (Muṇḍ 1.2). The most that these virtues can do for one is to better his state in the next existence, but they cannot bring him to that highest goal (CU 5.10.7; Śvet 5.11, 12; KU 5.7; Muṇḍ 1.2). Knowledge is extolled as the means, but this is not lower knowledge, neither the little knowledge that is a dangerous thing nor the "much learning" that Festus told Paul had made him mad (Acts 26:24). Such knowledge is no more than a variety of ignorance, and the worst variety at that (BAU 4.4.10; Īśā 9; cf. KU 2.23–25). The knowledge needed is true knowledge, the higher knowledge, the knowledge of metaphysical truth, which leads one to the goal (Kena 1.4–8).

The first requisite for attainment of the higher knowledge, as we have already seen, is extinction of desire (BAU 4.4.6; Tait 2.1; KU 3.7–8). A man's purpose must be single. Mere abstinence from evil conduct is not sufficient, though it is a precondition (KU 2.24). The knower of Brahman rises above considerations of good and evil (Muṇḍ 3.1–3; KU 2.14; 5.11). He must, indeed, rise above all the pairs of opposites including the pair that is most fundamental and is of the largest dimensions. For late in the Upanishadic period the Real, which is Brahman or Ātman, is stated to include both the Sat and the Asat (Muṇḍ 2.21). Everything is unified and transcended in it.

Thus there logically develops in the late Upanishadic period the doctrine of Māyā or illusion, which continues to this day in much of traditional Hindu thinking.

According to it all sense experience and all phenomenal manifestations are not true in an absolute sense, but are only relatively true, being the product of the illusion-maker (*māyin,* Śvet 4.9). That curtain of illusion must be penetrated to find the Real.

Secondly, a seeker must have no attachments to distract him. He must renounce possessions, even family. He should not undertake self-support, but must live by begging. This is a kind of passive or negative begging, not active solicitation. He waits for people to give him the bare necessities of life. He provides them with the opportunity to acquire merit by making a gift to a person devoted to realizing the absolute. He does not ask for alms; he merely accepts them.

After the extinction of desire and renunciation of all attachments comes concentration upon his goal, and this means employment of meditation (Muṇḍ 2.2.3–4). For success in this the chief aid is use of Yoga, a technique—how ancient we do not know—for controlling the senses and mind, which are all physical, so that they will not interfere with the Soul's realization of itself (KU 2.12, 3.13, 6.11; Śvet 1.3, 2.8–13; Maitri 6.18–30). Yoga is even now so esteemed and utilized in India.

Idealistic epistemological monism is the chief development in the Upanishads, but it is not the only one. The dualistic view of the universe which we have seen in the Rig Veda continues into the Upanishads (Śvet; Maitri). In the Śvetāśvatara Upanishad there is also asserted an idea of great importance which has been hardly more than implied or hinted in earlier texts. This is the doctrine of loving devotion (*bhakti*) to God. In the final stanza of that work is the declaration: "Whoever has supreme devotion (*bhakti*) to God, and to his spiritual preceptor (*guru*) as to God, to him these matters which have been proclaimed become manifest if he be a great soul, yea, become manifest if he be a great soul." From now on, however, and above all in the Bhagavad Gītā and texts following it dedicated to worship of the god Vishnu and his incarnations (*avatāra*), Bhakti is of first importance. Through Bhakti, as through knowledge, one can, if he wins the god's grace, attain salvation, release from rebirth, and enjoy eternal supreme bliss.

The Bhagavad Gītā draws heavily upon the Upanishads and the Vedas and some other kinds of thinking as well, which are not clearly identifiable. It is not consistent in its viewpoint, but knows and uses monistic ideas, dualistic ideas, theistic ideas. It accepts the doctrine of rebirth and the effect of one's acts in determining the conditions of rebirth. It condemns desire and teaches renunciation in the name of God. Release from rebirth may be obtained through the performance of deeds without attachment to the results of the deeds, that is through the performance of them selflessly, without any emotional accompaniment, merely because one is doing his duty. Higher than this way to salvation is the way of knowledge, more difficult to achieve—only the rare person can expect to succeed through it. But the most feasible way is that of loving devotion (*bhakti*) to God. This is available to all, not merely to the ironwilled devotee of duty or to the superintellectual metaphysician, but to the lowly, the unsophisticated, the people of modest intelligence. Those who practice much devotion Krishna will accept. The simple heart is enough. By means of devotion one can gain the fullest knowledge, can know God, can win to Him. Such a one, in fact, has a special advantage. "I am the same to all beings," says Krishna, "there is no one either hateful to me or dear; but those who adore me with loving devotion, they are in me and I too in them" (BG 9.29).

No one should think that the pursuit of knowledge in India has been undertaken disinterestedly, for its own sake. There has always been some ulterior purpose prompting the search for the Real, and this is abundantly clear in the Rig Veda and the Upanishads. In hymn after hymn of the Rig Veda the rewards which the sacrificer expects are named—long life, prosperity, abundant lineage, victory over his enemies. In the Upanishads the fruit of knowledge is constantly specified. He who knows the truth about the nature of the fearless Brahman, himself becomes the fearless Brahman (BAU 4.4.25). He who knows the truth about the *arka* sacrificial fire and the horse sacrifice wards off the repetition of death (*punarmṛtyu:* BAU 1.2.7). He who knows the creation of the world from the unitary soul obtains the whole world (BAU 1.4.17). He who knows the teaching of the Kena Upanishad becomes established in the endless, heavenly world (Kena 34). Those who die having found the soul and their true desires, for them there is freedom to journey in all the worlds (CU 8.1.6). Throughout India's intellectual history knowledge gives power, a kind of power hard to view as being different from magic. To know a person's name is to have power over him. To know the secret of the universe is to have power over the universe and not to be bound any longer by it but to have it under one's own control. The aim of philosophic research in India has always been utilitarian. Her thinkers have sought the truth in the spirit of Christ when he said, "And ye shall know the truth, and the truth shall make you free" (John 8:32). The purpose of the search for the Real has been religious, and this idea is as firmly fixed in modern as it was in ancient India.

The various ideas described or mentioned in this brief presentation are those of the first thousand years of Indian speculative development. They have since then been the chief stimuli in Indian religious and philosophical speculation, leading to innumerable variations.

They start with the concrete naturalistic notions of the early Rig Veda, proceed to the first metaphysical speculations of the late Rig Veda, which are then elaborated in the Upanishads and the Bhagavad Gītā. They prepare the way for Jainism and Buddhism, and then the orthodox systems of philosophy, which proliferate endlessly in the inquiries and cult practises of mediaeval times and the still further refinements in post-mediaeval centuries to our own day. Taken all together these many ideas constitute an intellectual tree of immense growth and uncounted ramifications. There may be a graft here and there from outside, but in general there is an identifiable continuity. The end result is often enough very different from the beginning, may even be directly contradictory to it. The Rigvedic poet who celebrated Indra's victory over Vṛtra as the story of the origin and structure of the universe would have been astonished to hear such teaching as that of the great Shankara, exponent of an uncompromising idealistic monism in the eighth and ninth centuries A.D., some two thousand years later. He would doubtless have comprehended nothing of what Shankara said. Yet the connection is traceable. Step at a time the search for the Real had gone forward until it asserted reality for what Shankara's Rigvedic ancestor would have been likely to consider only the most insubstantial and vaporous of imaginings. He would not have believed that a tree sprung from early Vedic belief as the seed could produce such strange fruit.

Through the whole millennium of India's intellectual development discussed here, there was a constant willingness of her thinkers to listen to new ideas. The tone of the late Rigvedic speculations and of the Upanishadic teachings is tentative and undogmatic. An idea which is advanced may be discussed and accepted, but before long it may be casually discarded in favor of some new idea that seems more plausible. There is here a tradition of speculation, teaching, belief, development, fresh approach, advance, which cannot fail to win our admiration. It has set a pattern for later Indian religious development. Heresy has hardly been known in the native Indian tradition, and persecution for novel or startling ideas has been a rarity. Mutually contradictory doctrines have been allowed, and are still allowed, to stand side by side in argumentative and unreconciled, but not violently hostile, coexistence. There has been an amazing willingness to tolerate another's opinion on intellectual issues, though it may differ from one's own, on the generally accepted theory that no one of us has found the final word, knows the ultimate truth. Even the great teachers, to whom revelation was thought to have come by some mystic experience, were contradicted by other great teachers similarly venerated, and the followers of each let the followers of the others live and preach and worship for the most part unmolested. Ultimate truth, the absolute Real, it seems, may be fleetingly, mistily glimpsed vanishing somewhere over the crest of a remote hill or just slipping around some distant curve, ever remaining the object of possibly futile, but certainly unremitting, pursuit, while what has been left behind, which yesterday was thought might be the Real, has today become only the abandoned Unreal.

2.
The Unity of Life

If we were to ask a devout Christian and a devout Hindu who one's brother is, we would expect very different answers. The Christian view is that one's brother is his fellow man, or, as it is put in both the Old and New Testament, his neighbor is his fellow man, whom he should love as himself (Lev. 19.18; Matt. 19.19 and 22.39; Mark 12.33). To illustrate this view the Christian might cite the parable of the good Samaritan (Luke 10.29–37), which has a moral that was apparently questionable to Jesus' audience as being extreme, too latitudinarian. But to the Hindu the Christian definition would appear narrow, restrictive, and therefore indefensible and untenable. The Hindu considers that one's brother or neighbor is not merely humankind but the lower animals as well. He recognizes that all life is a unity. This view is now, and for two millennia or more has been, a feature of Hinduism, Jainism, and Buddhism, the three great religions that are native to India. As a common Indian value, held to be valid in both traditional and modern India, it has had important intellectual and ethical consequences and ramifications, and prompts interesting questions. It is the purpose of this lecture to examine some of the history of the idea, observe some of its consequences and ramifications, and consider some of the questions it raises.

The most important consequence is the ethical precept that one should not inflict injury upon any living creature. It is a matter of simple logic that belief in the unity of life should lead to the doctrine that wherever life exists, it should be inviolable. The Indian term for the doctrine is Ahinsa (*ahiṃsā*), which is variously translated as "harmlessness, noninjury, nonviolence," the last being Gandhi's rendering. The word *ahiṃsā* is Sanskrit and is a negative formation, made by prefixing the negative element *a-* to the noun *hiṃsā* which means "injury." Hence *ahiṃsā* means non-*hiṃsā,* the opposite of *hiṃsā* or "injury." But though the term Ahinsa is negative in formation, the idea it expresses is positive, for it includes the practise of "friendliness" (*maitrī*) and "compassion" (*karuṇā*). Ahinsa is the most important and most widely preached of all Indian ethical teachings, and the three faiths unite in supporting the frequently quoted Sanskrit aphorism *ahiṃsā paramo dharmaḥ,* "Ahinsa is the highest religion," which is often reinforced by the statement that however much religions may differ on other points, they agree on this. Gandhi expressed that view in different phraseology when he said, "I am fascinated by the law of love. It is the philosopher's stone for me. I know that Ahinsa alone can provide a remedy for our ills."

Many kinds of persuasion are used in the traditional literature of Buddhism, Jainism, and Hinduism to support the teaching of Ahinsa. Often the method is direct exhortation in sermons; often—and perhaps more effectively—it is by the use of exempla to illustrate the rewards of practicing Ahinsa or the retribution for violating it. A kind act to an animal, especially an act that involves self-denial or pain for the doer, may be shown to bring one a happier lot in a future existence. On the other hand, injury of an animal may lead to condign punishment. A Buddhist story (Jātaka 18) which includes a sectarian sideswipe at Brahmanical Hinduism, illustrates this.

A Brahman was preparing to make an offering to his dead ancestors by sacrificing a goat, and had turned the animal over to his disciples for the preliminary bathing and garlanding. While this was going on, the goat suddenly acquired recollection of its previous existences and thereupon burst into a loud peal of laughter, like the breaking of a pot. But a moment later it fell into a fit of weeping. The disciples reported this unprecedented behavior to the Brahman, who asked the goat, "Why did you laugh?" "Because," replied the goat, "long ago in a previous existence I was a Brahman like you and I too celebrated just such a sacrifice to the dead. As a result I was doomed to be reborn as a goat for 500 successive existences, and in each existence to have my head cut off. I have already suffered this fate 499 times, and now when my head is cut off for the 500th time, my punishment will come to an end. Therefore in my joy I laughed." "And why," asked the Brahman, "did you weep?" "I wept," said the goat, "when I thought of the 500 existences of sorrow which you are about to bring upon yourself by cutting off my head." "Never fear," said the Brahman, "I shall not sacrifice you and you shall escape the pain of having your head cut off." "It will make no difference for you to spare me," said the goat, "my head must inevitably be cut off." The Brahman, however, gave orders to his disciples to see that no harm came to the goat. Once free, the goat ran over to a ledge of rock and stretched its head out to nibble the leaves on a bush growing there. At that moment out of the clear sky came a sudden bolt of lightning, which split off a sliver from the overhanging rock, and this sliced off the goat's outstretched head as clean as with an executioner's knife.

Besides supporting Ahinsa with threats of disastrous consequences, the religious literature has many legends to illustrate the theme that the genuinely good and wise practise Ahinsa as a positive virtue. One such legend among the Jains is that of Nemi, the twenty-second of the twenty-four world Saviors who that faith says have appeared successively in the past billions of years to teach mankind the eternal truth and the way to gain release from the otherwise beginningless and endless round of rebirths.

Nemi is said in the legend to have been born a prince, as were all the Jain Saviors, and was raised in comfort and splendor. He is represented as a contemporary and cousin of the Hindu hero and teacher Krishna, who is an incarnation (*avatāra*) of the god Vishnu and the reciter of the Bhagavad Gītā. After Nemi as a wonder child and gifted youth had performed a number of marvelous feats, his father wanted him to marry, but Nemi, already obsessed with following the call of religion, demurred. The king then asked Krishna to use his influence on him, and Krishna turned the assignment over to his wives. They joked Nemi at having reached marriageable age but remaining unwed. He answered that there was no profit in associating with women and getting married; he preferred to seek perfection and release from rebirth. Then Krishna himself spoke to Nemi, reminding him that all previous world Saviors had married and raised families before abandoning worldly affairs to follow the quest of religion. He should therefore marry and please his father. Nemi reluctantly consented, and a beauteous bride was selected for him, the daughter of a neighboring king and Nemi's wife in previous existences. On the appointed day, the bride, bathed and adorned, and filled with agitation and delight at securing so rare a bridegroom, was seated in a splendidly decorated marriage pavilion waiting for Nemi. He, too, fully ornamented, was on his way, riding in a noble chariot. But suddenly he heard a confused hullabaloo of piteous cries. He looked around and saw that the cries came from a pen filled with fowl, deer, and other animals waiting to be slaughtered for the wedding feast. The thought of their imminent death revolted him, and filled with disgust at the worldly life and now solidly confirmed in his intent to seek the goal of religion, he stripped off his jewels and finery to give it all to his charioteer and ordered him to turn the chariot around and head for the open spaces. Thus he abandoned his unclaimed bride so that he could become a houseless mendicant wanderer searching for salvation. In the sequel the bride also became an ascetic successfully seeking release from the misery of rebirth. The story of Nemi is one of the best-loved in all Jain hagiography, and it is copiously told in literary texts, illustrated in miniature paintings, and carved in wood and stone in temples. It moves the compassionate heart of Jainism and emphasizes for Jains the brotherhood of man with the subhuman creation.

Belief in the inviolability of all life naturally leads to the practice of vegetarianism. Meat-eating is abhorred today by strict Jains and Hindus and many Buddhists much as cannibalism is by us. The prohibition extends even to the eating of eggs or any dishes made with eggs. In our time the practice of vegetarianism as an accompaniment to the practice of Ahinsa was an ethical essential in Gandhi's program. He demanded a vow of Ahinsa and vegetarianism from all those who came to live in his hermitage (*āshram*) and continually preached the doctrine in his speeches and writing.

For Hindus today and for a good many centuries in

the past, perhaps for as much as two millennia, the doctrine of Ahinsa has reached its apex with respect to the cow. That animal has for them a special sanctity, entitling it not only to protection and inviolability but to actual worship as well. Since the arrival of the Muslims in India, first in the eighth century, the cow has continouusly been one of the chief causes of quarrels and bloody riots between Hindus and Muslims, for the latter, like Christians, have no feeling that the cow is sacred and instead slaughter it and eat its flesh. To Gandhi the cow was "a poem of pity," and cow-protection was a fundamental item in his program for the regeneration of India. He always wanted it to be a goal of nationalism. His insistence upon the point, like that of the great nationalist leader Tilak before him, was never considered reasonable or even intelligible or tolerable by Muslims and was an important factor in the failure of the Indian National Congress to get full Muslim cooperation in the struggle against the British. After the attainment of Independence, when a new constitution was adopted in 1950, one of the directive principles of state policy prescribed that the government is to prevent "slaughter of cows and calves, and other milch and draught cattle"—a provision that may or may not have been included partly for economic reasons but certainly was a concession to Hindu religious sensibilities. A number of Indian states today have cow-protection provisions; some prohibit the slaughter of old and decrepit cattle and support at public expense refuges or sanctuaries (*gosadan*) for them. There are a number of voluntary associations propagandizing for prohibition of cow slaughter in those states where it is permitted.

Questions naturally come to one's mind concerning the origin of the various ideas that all life, human and animal, is a unity; that all life, again both human and animal, is inviolable; and that for Hindus the cow is especially inviolable, that it is in fact sacred and to be worshipped. Let me start in considering these questions by surveying the data which Indian literature offers us concerning the unity of human and animal life. A basis for this belief appears first in connection with the doctrine of rebirth, also variously known as transmigration, metempsychosis, the round of existence.

The idea of repeated birth, rebirth, appears first in the Upanishads, at a time presumably some hundreds of years later than the compilation of the Rig Veda. It is preceded by the idea of repeated death (*punarmṛtyu*), which is mentioned in the Brāhmaṇas (Tait Brāh. 3.11.8.6. Kauṣ. Brāh. 2.5.1), the stratum of literature immediately following the four basic Vedas (Rig Veda, Yajur Veda, Sāma Veda, Atharva Veda) and preceding the Upanishads. In the Rig Veda the teaching about life after death seems to be that one who has performed his ritual duties and laid up treasure for himself in the next world by the offerings he has made on earth and the worship he has performed enjoys eternal happiness in the heaven at the top of the sky which is ruled by the god Varuṇa and Yama, the first man. Then the idea seems to develop that such a life also must terminate, or at least is liable to terminate unless some special means is found to prevent such termination. Hence in the Upanishads we find repeated death mentioned as something which the possessor of certain kinds of knowledge can ward off (BAU 1.2.7 and 1.5.2).

Discussion of the idea of rebirth appears first in an account found in two of the oldest Upanishads (BAU 6.2; CU 5.3–10), and it is taught not by a member of the priestly group, a Brahman, but by a Kshatriya, a member of the warrior, or ruling, class. The first account is less full than the second, giving only a part of the story. Śvetaketu, a well-known Upanishadic seeker of metaphysical knowledge and the son of another famous teacher, once went to a gathering of the princely Panchālas (*pañcāla*) and presented himself to one of them (Pravāhana Jaibali), presumably thinking that as a Brahman he would be asked to perform a sacrifice in behalf of that prince or to instruct him and would thus get a reward. Such was the accepted relationship of the Brahman, who was of the spiritual aristocracy, with the prince or *Kshatriya,* who was of the temporal aristocracy. The prince asked Śvetaketu, "Have you been instructed by your father?" "Yes," answered Śvetaketu. Thereupon the prince asked Śvetaketu a series of five questions which were: "Know you how people here, on dying, separate in different directions? . . . How they come back again to this world, . . . Why yonder world is not filled up with the many who go there from here, . . . In which oblation, when it is offered, the water becomes the person's voice, rises up, and speaks? . . . How one gets access to the path leading to the gods, or to the one leading to the fathers, so that, by doing what, people go to the path of the gods or to that of the fathers?" "Not a single one of them do I know," Śvetaketu admitted frankly. The prince, nevertheless, asked him to remain, but Śvetaketu, appalled by his own ignorance, ran off to his father to complain that he had been imperfectly instructed and repeated the five questions to him. The latter also frankly admitted that he too, did not know the answers, and then went to the prince, who received him hospitably as a Brahman and offered him a boon. He chose the answers to the questions which the prince had put to Śvetakteu. The prince, trying to put him off, replied, "That is among divine boons. Ask me a human boon." The Brahman replied that he had all the possessions he needed and besought the prince to be generous and give him the answers to the five questions. The prince then told him to seek instruction in the usual manner, that is, as a pupil, apparently expecting that the Brahman would be too proud to become a pupil of a non-Brahman. But the Brahman came to him with fuel for the sacrificial fire in his hand, which was the conventional symbolic way of offering oneself as a pupil. The prince then yielded. The knowledge, he said, had previously been an esoteric possession of the warrior class and had never been imparted to a Brahman, but he would communicate it to him, though a Brahman, since he could not refuse one who came as a pupil.

The part of the prince's communication which is pertinent here is as follows. When a man dies and his body is being burned, the man—by which is meant the life that is in the man—arises having the color (appearance) of light. The life of those who know this and those who truly worship faith (*śraddhā*) passes from the flame of the cremation fire into the day, from the day into the half month of the waxing moon, from there to the six months of the year during which the sun progresses northward, from there into the world of the gods (*devaloka*), from therc into the sun, and from there into the lightning-fire. From there it is led into the worlds of *brahman,* which is the mystic force in the universe, the Absolute. Here it dwells for long periods, and never returns.

But the life of those who conquer the world by sacrificial offerings (cf. Muṇḍ 1.2), charity, and austerity rather than by the worship of faith passes into the smoke of the cremation fire; from the smoke into the night, from the night into the half month of the waning moon, then into the six months when the sun moves southward, then to the world of the fathers, from there to the moon. There those dead become food, and the gods feed upon them. When that food passes away for the gods, the transmigrating lives pass forth into space, from there into air, then into rain, and then into the ground. There they become food through being plants. They are consumed by men, pass as semen into women, and are born. Thus they rise up again in this world, and repeat the cycle. "But," the text adds ominously, "those who know not these two ways become crawling and flying insects and whatever there is here that bites."

This is a theory of transmigration in which the conditions of rebirth are determined solely by one's knowledge. Nothing is said about one's action (*karma*) as a determinant. But in the other version of this episode (CU 5.3–10), action (*karma*) is mentioned as the controlling element. The text says that for those who are of pleasant conduct here the prospect is that they will enter a pleasant womb, either the womb of a Brahman, or the womb of a Kshatriya, or the womb of a Vaishya. But those who are of stinking conduct here—the prospect is that they will enter a stinking womb, either the womb of a dog, or the womb of a swine, or the womb of a *caṇḍāla* (an untouchable).

A third passage (KU 1.2) simplifies the progression from death to rebirth and makes it apply more generally. When people die, they all go to the moon. During its earlier (waxing) period, the moon nourishes itself with their breathing spirits (*prāṇa*); with its latter (waning) period it causes them to be reproduced. This, that is, the moon, is the door of the heavenly world. Whoever answers it, the moon permits to go farther. But whoever does not answer, the moon sends down to earth as rain. Either as a worm, or as a moth, or as a fish, or as a bird, or as a lion, or as a wild boar, or as a snake, or as a tiger, or as a person, or as some other, in this or that condition, he is born again on earth according to his deeds (*karma*), according to his knowledge (cf. CU 6.9.3). If he has knowledge of *brahman* he enters the way that leads to the world of *brahman* and so terminates rebirth. In this version knowledge and action join to determine the conditions of rebirth.

Still more flatly in another passage *karma* (action) is specified as the sole determinant of rebirth and knowledge as the source of release from it (BAU 4.4.3ff) : at death the soul, like a caterpillar in passing from one blade of grass to another, draws itself together, strikes down this body, dispels its ignorance, and makes for itself a newer and better form. According as one acts, so he becomes. Whatever is his desire, whatever he is attached to, that he becomes. But he who knows the Ātman, the imperishable, at death goes to the *brahman*-world, becomes *brahman*, and is not born again.

These are the earliest recorded speculations about rebirth. Some of them make no allusion to rebirth in animal form, and one may reasonably think that such a possibility had not been universally accepted by the early Upanishadic thinkers. Further, some of the theorizing, as we have seen, leads the transmigrating soul on an involved course before it either reaches its final blissful eternal state or is reborn on earth. Only the last passage quoted deals with rebirth as a direct transition from one body to another, as is the usual assumption of Jainism, Buddhism, and Hinduism.

Though the Upanishads contain the first literary references to the idea of rebirth and to the notion that one's action (*karma*) determines the conditions of one's future existences, and though they arrive at the point of recognizing that rebirth may occur not only in human form but also in animal bodies, they tell us nothing about the precept of Ahinsa. Yet that precept is later associated with the belief that a soul in its wandering may inhabit both kinds of forms. Ancient Brahmanical literature is conspicuously silent about Ahinsa. The early Vedic texts do not even record the noun *ahiṃsā* "noninjury" nor know the ethical teaching which the noun later designates. The first occurrence of the word in Sanskrit literature is in the Upanishads, but there it occurs only once (CU 3.17.4) and in a context that has nothing to do with transmigration. It is merely mentioned inconspicuously in a list of five virtues, and without any indication of its character. These virtues are austerity (*tapas*), almsgiving (*dāna*), rectitude (*ārjava*), Ahinsa (noninjury, *ahiṃsā*), and truthfulness (*satyavacana*). It is evident that these are prized virtues or virtuous practices, but nothing is said about them. All of them except Ahinsa are mentioned elsewhere in the Upanishads, some of them frequently, but Ahinsa stands here isolated and unexplained. Nor is an explanation of Ahinsa deducible from other parts of Vedic literature. The ethical concept which it embodies was entirely foreign to the thinking of the early Vedic Aryans, who recognized no kinship between human and animal creation, but rather ate meat and offered animals in the sacrifices to the gods.

When we pass beyond Vedic literature we find the idea of Ahinsa only slowly winning status in Brahmanical circles. We may start with the Bhagavad Gītā, which calls itself an Upanishad, has in many respects a great deal of similarity to the Upanishads, and is probably not very remote from those texts in time. The Bhagavad Gītā mentions the doctrine of Ahinsa in four passages. Two of these are lists of virtues, in one case nineteen in number (10.4–5), in the other twenty-six (16.1–3). In a third passage the word appears in a list of nineteen heads of knowledge (13.7–11). In the fourth it is included among five austerities of the body (17.14). As was the case with the Upanishadic passage in which Ahinsa is listed, so too in the Bhagavad Gītā there is no intimation of the content of the doctrine, that is, the range of its applicability, whether to all animate beings or to men alone, and we are left to make our own guess. We may assume in any case that no really great emphasis was put upon it, for the immediate purpose of the Bhagavad Gītā seems to be opposed to the teaching of Ahinsa as it is later understood. As the late Professor Franklin Edgerton remarks in the introductory essay to his translation of the Bhagavad Gītā: "The Gītā's morality on this point is somewhat disappointing. It does include 'harmlessness' or 'nonviolence' (*ahiṃsā*) in several of its lists of virtues. But it never singles it out for special emphasis . . . some lip-homage is paid to it. But it is never definitely and sharply applied in such a form as 'Thou shalt not kill.'"[1]

Somewhat later than the Bhagavad Gītā is the legal text ascribed to Manu, which is the most highly valued of Hindu legal texts and is usually considered to be an accretion of material made during the two centuries before the beginning of the Christian era and the two centuries following it. On the subject of Ahinsa the text is equivocal. It contains various passages which specifically endorse Ahinsa (e.g., 2.177; 10.63; 11.159). Another passage says that he who eats the meat of any animal in this world will be eaten by that same animal in yonder world (5.55). But there are also passages which are permissive on meat-eating: for example, one of them classifies animals into those which may and those which may not be eaten (5.11 ff.). Another says: "One should eat flesh which has been consecrated, and at the desire of Brahmans, and when dully required, and in danger of life. Prajāpati made all this food for life; both movable and immovable, all is food for life. The immovable are food of those that move about; the toothless of those with teeth (or fangs); those without hands, or those with; the timid (such as deer), of the bold (such as the tiger). An eater who even day by day eats living beings is not polluted, for the eatable living beings were created by the Creator as well as eaters" (5.27–30). Other passages contradicting Ahinsa could be quoted.

Manu's laws take the general position that one should eat consecrated flesh, that is, flesh which has been offered in sacrifice, but not unconsecrated (5.36–38). If one eats what has been consecrated, he does good both to himself and the animal which has been slain (5.39–42). But if he does not eat it, he will be reborn as a beast for twenty-one existences (5.35). Other legal texts following that of Manu are also equivocal.

The Arthaśāstra, a Hindu treatise on government usually regarded as having a core which comes from the fourth or third century B.C. but as having reached its present textual state probably in the fourth century A.D., recognizes the sale of meat as legal but requires butchers to see that the meat is fresh (2.26). In the great epic, the Mahābhārata, which is another text built up through centuries by a steady process of accretion, there are many passages commanding observance of Ahinsa, yet elsewhere in that work meat-eating is mentioned only casually, and the existence of a butcher shop is not considered shocking (3.207).[2]

The double doctrine of Ahinsa and vegetarianism has never had full and unchallenged acceptance and practise among Hindus, and should not be considered to have arisen in Brahmanic circles. It seems more probable that it originated in a non-Brahmanical environment, was promoted in historic India by the Jains and the Buddhists, and was adopted by Brahmanic Hinduism after it began to win its way in north India, where Brahmanic Hinduism was developed.[3] But even in Jainism and Buddhism it was not fully established in their earliest period, if we are to judge from the evidence of texts. Further evidence of noncompliance appears in historical records. When the great emperor Ashoka was converted to Buddhism (ca. 262 B.C.), he became a strict adherent to the doctrine of Ahinsa and endeavored to enforce it in a set of rules which are recorded in his Pillar

Edict V and appointed officers to enforce it and other moral legislation (Rock Edicts V, XII; Pillar Edict VII). It is doubtful that he was very successful, for the Pali Buddhist texts show that hunting, trapping, and slaughtering were recognized occupations, with shops to handle their wares.[4] Some sixty years after Ashoka's death the Hindu dynasty of the Śungas and following that the Andhra dynasty are said to have reinstituted the old Vedic animal sacrifices.[5] Later, in mediaeval India, the doctrine of Ahinsa, though supported by Hinduism, Jainism, and Buddhism, was obviously hard to enforce. The Buddhist emperor Harsha, who ruled a large empire in northern India in the seventh century (A.D. 606–647), imposed penalties for its violation, which, according to the Chinese Buddhist pilgrim Hsüan-tsang, who visited India 630–644, extended to punishment by death. Half a millennium later King Kumārapāla, a convert to Jainism, who ruled a moderately good-sized kingdom in Western India in the twelfth century (A.D. 1142–1172), is reported in Jain literature to have been a savage partisan of Ahinsa. For example, he is said to have inflicted the death penalty upon an unlucky merchant who was discovered in possession of meat near a sanctuary in his capital city. Mediaeval Hindu rulers in Kashmir, according to Kalhaṇa, the great chronicler of Kashmirian history, also endeavored to enforce Ahinsa whenever they felt secure enough to make the attempt (e.g., Rājataranginī 3.5–6; 5.119).

When we turn to the development of the doctrine that the cow has special sanctity, we deal with a more limited segment of Indian religious authority and practise than when we investigate the wider doctrine of Ahinsa, for the sanctity of the cow is specifically a notion of Hinduism. It is so much a part of Hinduism today that J. N. Farquhar, a distinguished modern authority, could say that caste, rebirth, and the sanctity of the cow are the principal tenets of Hinduism on the popular level.[6] Jainism and Buddhism, however, give the cow no special preference over other animals in the implementation of Ahinsa. For them the slaying of any other creature—goat, dog, bird, or whatever it may be—is just as reprehensible as the slaying of a cow, and brings just as dire retribution.

The idea of the sanctity of the cow originated in the environment of the Rig and Atharva Vedas and I believe may fairly be regarded as a creation, to some extent unconscious, of the Brahman priesthood.[7] At least three items in Vedic religion seem to me to have combined to give the cow its exalted sacred position. To them were added in post-Vedic times the support of two wider Indian doctrines originating in a non-Vedic environment, namely, the doctrine of Ahinsa and the still more ancient belief in the mother goddess, with which the cow came to be identified. The three Vedic items gave the cow a status of sanctity but without inviolability; the two later notions from non-Vedic sources seem to have given it inviolability.

The first of the three Vedic items is the importance of the cow and its products in Vedic economic life and the value that animal therefore acquired in the Vedic sacrificial ritual. Cattle or herds of cattle or the products of the cow are the standard items mentioned in descriptions of wealth. Cattle constituted the great booty in war. No other animal had comparable economic value. This made it and its products the best of offerings to the divine figures whom the Vedic ritual was meant to propitiate. Further, in Vedic literature no other animal figures so frequently in simile or metaphor applied to a wide range of religious subjects—the phenomena of nature, such as dawn, the rays of morning light, rainfall or streams; deities, both male and female; human beings; the paraphernalia of the sacrifice, such as the stones for pressing out the sacred drink called *soma,* whose sound as they rub together may be called the bellowing of bulls, or the *soma* drops used in the oblation, which also may be called bulls because of their power.

There is, however, no hint here that the animal was also held inviolable. On the contrary, the animal sacrifice is a well-established feature of the Vedic religion, and the priests ate the flesh after it had been offered. Further, the cow was regularly used as food in circumstances calling for elaborate entertainment. The eating of meat seems, indeed, to have been a common enough occurrence in Vedic society for those who could afford it. A passage recommends the yearly performance of the animal sacrifice, which the text says means "cattle," to perpetuate the sacrificer's own herds, for, says the text, "flesh is the best kind of food."

The second of the three Vedic items is the figurative use in Vedic literature of words for cow, bull, ox, herds of cows. No symbol of fecundity or maternity or source of nourishment compares in the Veda to the cow. No symbol of virility compares to the bull. Any female at all, whether a deity like Ushas (the Dawn), or a cosmic element like the Waters (*āpas*), or a human queen, or just a beautiful young woman (RV 10.95.6), seems flattered if she is called a cow or compared to a cow or characterized as a mother of cows (RV 4.52.2). And a heroic god like Indra or Agni, or a human king is gratified to be lauded as a bull. The very gods are said to be born of a cow (*gojāta*). Some of the applications of words for cow or bull should be mentioned specifically. One of these is the characterization of the seven cosmic Waters (*āpas*) as cows. Their part in the creation myth was mentioned in the preceding lecture. They had been confined by the demon Vṛtra, and when the god Indra slew Vṛtra, out they flowed, thus providing the moisture needed for creation. Marvelously, too, they proved to be jointly pregnant, and their embryo was the Sun, which furnished the universe with light and heat. The rain clouds may be called cows, and they have a calf which is the lightning. And Agni, the priest-god of the Vedic sacrifice and the counterpart on earth of the lightning in the atmosphere and the sun in the sky, is called "Child of the Waters" (*apāṃ napāt*) or calf (*vatsa*). All life depends upon the Waters. They purify their worshipper and give healing, both physical and moral. They are, in short, both sanctified and sanctifying, and when they are called cows, as they are too many times to count, they invest the cow, at least for the time being, with a part of their sanctity.

The rays of light at dawn are frequently called a herd of cows. The deified Dawn is herself many times called a cow. These cows again are especially sanctified, for they refer to the first rays of light that usher in the day and inaugurate the sacrificial ritual, so important for the welfare of gods, men, and the universe. Not least of all they bring to the priests who perform the sacrifice their fee, which is called *dakṣiṇā* [*go*] "the cow that is able to calve and give milk"—in this connection we might render the word *dakṣiṇā* as "Liberality," or simply "Priest's Fee." [8]

Other feminine religious figures of the highest importance to Vedic man, who receive the epithet of cow, include Aditi, the personification of a pure abstraction, whose name means "boundlessness, freedom, expansion." She is the spirit of creation, development, evolution. A hymn says she is "the sky, the atmosphere, the mother, the father, the son, all the gods and the five folk; Aditi is what is born; Aditi is what is to be born" (RV 1.89.10). Since her name means "freeing" she acquires a moral function and is conceived as freeing from sin. She is a milch cow (*dhenu*) "who issues full streams [of blessings] for pious folk who make the oblation" (RV 1.153.3). In the *soma* ceremony her name (*aditi*) is used as an epithet of that cow whose daughters are the milk sought by the masculine element *soma,* here compared to a tawny bellowing bull inflamed with lust. In the performance of the Vedic ritual she is symbolized by a cow. The earth is another feminine entity which comes to be identified with Aditi and under the name Pṛthivī (the Wide One) or Mahī (the Great One) is called a cow (e.g. RV 4.41.5; 10, 133.7; possibly 10.67.5; 10.101.9). The equation in Vedic literature of Aditi, Earth, and cow is recognized in the early commentary on Vedic words by Yāska called Naighaṇṭuka (1.1.4–5; 2.3.16), where the word *go,* "cow," is synonymous with many things, including earth, heaven, the ritual utterance (Vāc), Aditi. The use of the word or words for "cow" had by then grown from a descriptive figure of speech applied in compliment to feminine entities until it had become a symbol of the holiest of those entities and had finally won identity with them. They were cows, and the cow was they. The metaphor or symbol had got away from those who employed it. They had ceased to distinguish it from the object it had been meant to adorn or to represent, and the cow had acquired their holiness as a property of itself. Thus came about the apotheosis of the cow.

The third item in Vedic times conducing to the cow's sanctity was the Brahman's jealousy of his rights in respect to ownership of cows. We have already noted how responsive the Vedic priests were to their fee, which was a cow or cows. The literature has many references to the Brahman's cow, his inalienable right to claim and keep it, the fearful punishment that will befall one who withholds it or takes it away from him. In the hymns Aditi as the holy cosmic cow is equated with the Brahman's cow, and in a threatening passage of the Rig Veda she is made to say: "Me, who know the ritual spell, who raise up the sacrificial voice (*vāc*) inherent in all pious devotions, a goddess arrived from the gods, me, the cow, the mortal of small intelligence has appropriated as his own" (RV 8.101.15–16). There are four full hymns in the Atharva Veda which denounce in the strongest terms that person, normally a king, who would take or injure the Brahman's cow, in a wider sense any of a Brahman's property which was represented as a whole by the cow as the symbol of wealth (AV 5.18; 5.19; 12.4; 12.5). Let me quote a few stanzas from the late Maurice Bloomfield's spirited translation.[9]

With his offspring does he trade, of his cattle is he deprived, that refuses to give the cow of the gods to the begging descendants of the Ṛṣis.

Through (the gift of) a cow with broken horns his (cattle) breaks down, through a lame one he tumbles into a pit, through a mutilated one his house is burned, through a one-eyed one his property is given away.

For those that come requesting her the cow has been created by the gods. Oppression of Brahmans it is called, if he keeps her for himself.

The gods, O king, did not give thee this (cow) to eat. Do not, O prince, seek to devour the cow of the Brahman, which is unfit to be eaten!

The prince, beguiled by dice, the wretched one who has lost as a stake his own person, he may, perchance, eat the cow of the Brahman, (thinking) "let me live today (if) not tomorrow."

They who ruled over a thousand, and were themselves ten hundred, the Vaitahavya, when they devoured the cow of the Brahman, perished.

They who spat upon the Brahman, who desired tribute from him, they sit in the middle of a pool of blood, chewing hair.

A cruel (sacrilegious) deed is her slaughter; her meat,

when eaten, is sapless; when her milk is drunk, that surely is accounted a crime against the Fathers.

The *kūdī* plant (Christ's thorn) that wipes away the track (of death), which they fasten to the dead, that very one, O oppressor of Brahmans, the gods did declare (to be) thy couch.

The tears which have rolled from (the eyes of) the oppressed (Brahman), as he laments, these very ones, O oppressor of Brahmans, the gods did assign to thee as thy share of water.

The water with which they bathe the dead, with which they moisten his beard, that very one, O oppressor of Brahmans, the gods did assign to thee as thy share of water.

The rain of Mitra and Varuṇa does not moisten the oppressor of Brahmans; the assembly is not complacent for him; he does not guide his friend according to his will.

After hearing such curses, a king of Vedic times must have been a chilled and hardened atheist who withheld the cow that was due a Brahman or took it or any other property away from him.

It should be noted that, though the cow is sacred, it is not the cow's sanctity which is the issue here. The issue is that the cow is the Brahman's property. The wicked king's sin is not the taking of the cow's life; the sin lies in robbing the priesthood.

By the close of the Vedic period the literature shows that the sanctity of the cow was well established in Brahmanic teaching. But the cow had not yet acquired inviolability to injury. It was still offered as a sacrifical victim, and its flesh was still eaten. It was appreciated for its economic value and its use in the ritual magic of the sacrifice. It had also had so extensive a figurative use in application to divine feminine figures of the highest importance that the consciousness that the use was figurative had dimmed and passed away. These divine figures had been called cows so often that they were actually considered to be cows. In reverse the cow was considered to be those sacred figures and itself acquired their sanctity and the right to be worshipped. Coupled with this transfer of metaphor to acceptance as literal reality was the enhanced value attached to the status of the Brahman's cow and the fearful penalties falling from heaven upon him who killed or misappropriated it, all of which is illustrated in stories in the Mahābhārata, the Purāṇas, and other literature. The sanctions which applied to the Brahman's cow were ready at hand to be applied to cows as a zoological species.

At this time, that is, at the end of the Vedic period, the Brahmanic tradition was showing its first recognition of the doctrine of Ahinsa in the Upanishads and after them in the Bhagavad Gītā, though with no indication of the range of its application. This we have seen above. The doctrine, as it was being taught by the Jains and Buddhists, applied to all animals. But when Brahmanic Hinduism took it over, the exalted position which the cow had attained above all other animals gave it similar exaltation in the application of Ahinsa.

Just when the notion of the cow's sanctity became associated with the pre-Aryan conception of the Great Mother or Earth Goddess cannot be ascertained. The latter idea existed in the Harappa culture in the third millennium B.C.; a form of it appears in the Buddhist figure of Hāritī, known in sculpture from around the beginning of the Christian era; and it is widely associated with Tantric worship of the female element in Indian religions down to the present day. The Mother Goddess and Great Mother ideas have an ideological affinity with the Vedic goddesses Aditi, Pṛthivī (the Wide One), and Mahī (the Great One), that is, with the Earth goddess, who, as was mentioned above, is often called Cow. The

Vedic conception never blended fully and cleanly with the pre-Aryan or non-Aryan notions, but it did at least produce an identification of the universal Mother as a Cow. In recent times this led to a conception in religio-nationalist circles of the cow as the Indian motherland.

The history and basis of the Hindu doctrine that the cow is sacred and inviolable has been a kind of excursus from the main line of our discussion, which is the conception of life as a unity and its ideological consequences, but the importance of the cow's position has been such that the digression was justified, indeed was unavoidable. It has been possible, it seems to me, to answer our questions about the cow with a fair degree of plausibility—certainty would be too strong a word. In the case of Ahinsa, it is not possible to see the history of the idea so clearly, and the origin of the still wider idea, namely, that all life is a unity, is even more obscure. Nevertheless, I wish to make a few observations on those two subjects, and the discussion of them will conclude my remarks. We may perhaps use the method of working backward.

In the Upanishads, as we have seen, the doctrine of Ahinsa is a late arrival, and has an undefined content. That is also true in the Bhagavad Gītā. It seems clear that the idea would not have existed in those texts but for the belief in the doctrine of rebirth, when that belief came to include rebirth on earth in animal form as well as human form depending upon one's actions. But once the latter idea was accepted, namely, that transmigration carries an individual into all kinds of bodies, then it followed that human beings and animals were considered related, that basically they were identical, and that every living person has been an animal many times in the past and all but those rarest ones who succeed in escaping from the round of existence will be animals an indefinite number of times in the future. Hence human life and animal life are one, and it is apparent that we should treat animals with the same consideration that we show human beings. In so doing we satisfy our own ethical egoism.

All this sounds plausible enough, but I fear it is all only a chain of rationalization. The ideas of Ahinsa and the unity of all life did not have their origin in Vedic Aryan thought, but entered it from outside. The environment in which those ideas were at home was that of Jainism and Buddhism. In them Ahinsa was a dominant and original, not supplemental, feature. It was the first of the vows which every monk must take on entering the order of the two faiths, and its importance was developed in countless sermons in the earliest as well as the later strata of their literature. Jainism and Buddhism were wholeheartedly preaching Ahinsa at a time when it was only inconspicuously being accepted in the Upanishads and the Bhagavad Gītā. It is a good guess, having a high amount of probability, that the precept of Ahinsa and the doctrine of the unity of all life had their origin in non-Aryan culture, with which Aryan culture was blending at that time in northern India. Even if this be true, we still cannot see the origins of the ideas. I believe them to lie deep in prehistoric folk belief and agree with Professor Ludwig Alsdorf that Ahinsa is at bottom a magic-ritualistic tabu on taking life,[10] though, of course, there are no documents of the first half of the first millennium to prove this. So, too, we may not unreasonably regard the conception of the unity of life as being at base a generalized primitive folkloristic totemism, though again we cannot support such a view with substantiating documentation from the first millennium B.C. This pair of assumptions would provide an acceptable basis for the prevalence in India of the widespread belief in the unity of life as a religious axiom and the derivation from it of the doctrine of Ahinsa as the country's prime ethical value. Neither of the ideas is rational in the sense of being based upon processes of reasoning; rather they are congenital, inherent, visceral, emotional in their sources but at the same time all the stronger and more deeply rooted for being so, and the more likely, therefore, to extend their already long existence.

3.

Time Is a Noose

One of the historic religions of India tells of a distant golden age when all men were created good as well as equal, sickness did not exist, trees grew everywhere that granted people whatever they wished; rivers ran with wine; there was no strife, no hate, not even laws and rulers. But change is of the essence of our universe, and this order could not last. For more aeons than mortal mind can contemplate there has been a succession of time cycles, each with a period when the world steadily grew better until it reached perfection, followed by one when it became continuously worse until it reached the bottom, whereupon it started upward again. The golden age of the current cycle, when myth pictures so charming a consummation of philosophic anarchy, has gradually given way to the harsh realism of the present. The wishing-trees long ago ceased to bear fruit; the rivers stopped flowing with wine; people were no longer born as mutually congenial twins meant to be husband and wife in a wedlock free of contention. Patriarchs came to direct the folk; conduct had to be regulated by prohibitions, which at first consisted only of disapproving syllables, as one might say "Alas!" or "Fie!" As time grew worse, humankind demanded a king to settle disagreements, and the people chose a man of wisdom, who established laws and took the welfare of his subjects to heart in accordance with the Indian ideals of kingship as a benevolent paternalism. He instituted all the arts, including writing and arithmetic. When in the progressive deterioration people came to suffer from eating raw food, he invented pottery that they might have vessels in which to cook.

Having met the demands of material life, this same king became the first great religious of the cycle, discovering the way to salvation that rescues from the otherwise unending round of rebirth and proclaiming that way to mankind as the religion of Jainism. He was the first Savior in a world where corruption had set in, and in the billions of years since his time he has been followed by twenty-three others. By the time of the twenty-fourth, born only some 2,500 years ago, the world had reached so low a moral state that another Savior could not be born until the process of corruption should reach its lowest point and cease, some 40,000 years afterwards, and the world should start again on its upward course and advance to the level at which the last Savior had died.

To the Indian who accepts this or some similar tradition, no interpretation can be put upon material evolution except the pessimistic. It is the increasing evil of the world that demands a multiplication of social institutions and material objects, the development of science and invention. A complex civilization is merely a makeshift for facing an ever more painful existence. The occidental notion of evolution as a movement upwards is to him only a delusion; in a pre-Spenglerian way he sees it as a decline.

Yet such an Indian would not dispense with evolution; indeed he cannot, for he is powerless to check it. Not until the hand of the clock reaches the very bottom and starts upward can simplification be effected or even begun. In this present degenerate age when no one can hope for final salvation but at best may accomplish only some personal moral advance in each successive rebirth, an orderly and governed world makes for less painful existence. For we are all caught in the noose of time, from which the most prodigious effort can free no one until the thongs loosen of their own accord, whereupon by making such an effort a heroic soul can win escape.

Jainism, Buddhism, and Hinduism have all developed complex refinements of the cycle of time, but the roots of the idea seem to have been very simple. In the hymns of the Rig Veda, the poets confine their remarks about time to observable natural phenomena—the sequence of day and night, the movement of the sun and moon, the orderly procession of the months and the seasons, the succession of years. Men hope to live on earth for a hundred years, or to dwell in friendship with the god Varuṇa, who rules the realm of the blessed dead at the top of the universe "as long as days and dawns shall endure," as a stanza puts it (RV 7.88.4), a hope which we may fairly understand to mean forever. It is the recurrent sequence of days and nights and of other divisions of time that bring on old age and death. Such observations are all commonplace enough.

Curiosity did develop, however, about how mortality came into the world. We saw in the first lecture of this series (p. 26 above) that in one of the creation hymns (RV 10.72) an explanation is given. At the time of creation, when Aditi produced the seven gods known as Ādityas, she had an eighth son, Mārtāṇḍa, whose name means "one born of a dead egg," and him she cast aside. Possibly we should understand this to mean that she thought the egg sterile, or at least not able to hatch a god. This son was the Sun. He was, indeed, not capable of being an immortal god; rather, as the hymn states, Aditi bore him to be born and then to die again. Thus it was that mortality came into the world. Not only does the

Sun himself die every evening and have to be revived the next morning, but he has given the world days and nights, which measure man's life-span. He was also, it appears, the progenitor of the human race, for he figures in a rather complicated myth under a synonym (Vivasvant) and as such mated with Saraṇyū, daughter of Tvaṣṭṛ, the artificer of the gods. By her he had two pairs of twins. One pair were gods (the Aśvins) and hence immortal; but the other pair he had by her not in her true form but in a false counterfeit form (*savarṇā*), and they were Yama and Yamī, the first man and woman, the parents of the human race. Thus the Sun was the author of our mortality.

Time, in the form of the Year, is referred to mystically in the Rig Veda as a five-spoked wheel, on which "as it revolves all creations rest. Though heavy-laden its axle does not get heated. Even from yore the wheel with its years and with its nave has not been broken. Above the outstretched earth the wheel revolves, with its unaging felly" (RV 1. 164.13–14).

In the Atharva Veda Time (*kāla*) is a theme of philosophic speculation, and, as we saw in the first lecture, appears as one of the various ontological explanations offered by Vedic metaphysicians who were seeking to penetrate the mysteries of the cosmos. Time rolls on unceasingly, including within itself all that the universe contains; it is the creator. Even the self-existing one, the mystical power in the universe, is Time; from Time was born the creative heat or fervor evoked by the sacrifice. Two hymns make these asseverations with great positiveness (AV 19.53;19.54), and they are presented here in the vigorous translation of the late Professor Maurice Bloomfield,[1] with some minor changes.

Atharva Veda 19.53

1. Time, the steed, runs with seven reins (rays), thousand-eyed, ageless, rich in seed. The seers,

thinking holy thoughts, mount him, all the beings (worlds) are his wheels.

2. With seven wheels does this Time ride, seven naves has he, immortality is his axle. He carries hither all these beings (worlds). Time, the first god, now hastens onward.
3. A full jar has been placed upon Time; him, verily, we see existing in many forms. He carries away all these beings (worlds); they call him Time in the highest heaven.
4. He surely did bring hither all the beings (worlds), he surely did encompass all the beings (worlds). Being their father, he became their son; there is, verily, no other force, higher than he.
5. Time begot yonder heaven, Time also (begot) these earths. That which was, and that which shall be, urged forth by Time, spreads out.
6. Time created the earth, in Time the sun burns. In Time are all beings, in Time the eye looks abroad.
7. In Time mind is fixed, in Time breath (is fixed), in Time names (are fixed); when Time has arrived all these creatures rejoice.
8. In Time *tapas* (creative fervor) is fixed; in Time the highest (being is fixed); in Time *brahman* (the mystic power in the universe) is fixed; Time is the lord of everything, he was the father of Prajāpati.
9. By him this (universe) was urged forth, by him it was begotten. Time, truly, having become the *brahman* supports Parameṣṭhin (the highest lord).
10. Time created the creatures (*prajāḥ*), and Time in the beginning (created) the lord of creatures (Prajāpati); the self-existing Kaśyapa and the *tapas* (creative fervor) from Time were born.

Atharva Veda 19.54

1. From Time the waters did arise, from Time the *brahman* (the mystic power in the universe), the *tapas* (creative fervor), the regions (of space did arise). Through Time the sun rises, in Time he goes down again.

2. Through Time the wind blows, through Time (exists) the great earth; the great sky is fixed in Time. In Time the son (Prajāpati) begot of yore that which was, and that which shall be.
3. From Time the Ṛks (the sacred hymns) arose, the Yajus (the prose formula of the sacrifice) was born from Time; Time put forth the sacrifice, the imperishable share of the gods.
4. Upon Time the Gandharvas and Apsarases are founded, upon Time the worlds (are founded), in Time this Angiras and Atharvan rule over the heavens.
5. Having conquered this world and the highest world, and the holy (pure) worlds (and) their holy divisions; having by means of the *brahman* (the mystic power in the universe) conquered all the worlds, Time, the highest God, forsooth, hastens onward.

This rather simple, though impassioned, early affirmation of Time is a long way distant from the elaborately developed later cosmological systems of Jainism, Buddhism, and Hinduism, with their complex notions of Time, and the intervening stages of development of the conception of Time are not all evident to us, but we may look at the most striking of them which appear in the literature.

The idea of Time gets some relatively slight treatment in the Upanishads, where it is denied the status of first cause and instead holds a basic cosmological position similar to that which it has in later thinking. Two passages are pertinent. The deistic Śvetāśvatara Upanishad opens by addressing the cosmogonic question to those who know the mystical power of the universe (*brahmavid*) and suggests a series of possible answers. These start with Time (*kāla*) and go on with inherent nature (*svabhāva*), necessity (*niyati*), chance (*yadṛcchā*), the elements (*bhūta*), a womb (*yoni*), a male (*puruṣa*), the soul (*ātman*). But none of these is to be considered the first cause; rather the first cause is the self-power (*ātmaṣakti*) of God (*deva*), which is hidden in his own qualities (*guṇa*). He is the One who rules over all the possible causes just mentioned starting with "time" and ending with "the soul."

The other passage contains a more specific description of Time (Maitri 6.14), which in a prescientific age may have been considered to be using a rational or scientific, rather than subjective and metaphysical, method of analysis. The passage opens by reminding us that elsewhere the statement has been made that food is the source of this whole world, time is the source of food, and the sun is the source of time. The text then proceeds with an analysis of time in terms of the course which the sun follows during the year as it proceeds through the twenty-seven asterisms recognized by Hindu astronomy. Observation of the progressive and regular passage of the sun through them at the rate of two and one-quarter asterisms a month constitutes the proof, in fact the only proof, of time. Further, by recognizing the parts of time, from instants up to its greatest divisions, we can gain cognizance of time itself. But here we leave "science"—or proto-science—and turn to metaphysics. For beyond time, the text continues, is Brahman, the mystic power of the universe, and Brahman has two forms, namely, Time and beyond Time, the Timeless form. Time is the year, Prajāpati ("Lord of Creatures"), the Brahman-abode, the Ātman, the great ocean of creatures, the source of moon, stars, planets, the year, and the other things which we know, from all of which comes this whole world with whatever is good and evil in it. But Time is not the first cause. There is something else in which "Time is cooked," and this latter is Brahman, the Timeless. He who knows this profound truth, the text affirms, really knows the Veda.

In the Bhagavad Gītā nothing very different about

Time is added to the statements of the Upanishads. In a passage where Krishna, the god Vishnu incarnate, proclaims his universality by enumerating his many manifestations in a long series (10.19–42), he says that of measurers, those things which reckon by parts (as in the Maitri Upanishad quoted above), he is Time (10.30), and again that he is imperishable Time (10.33). Another view of Time in the Bhagavad Gītā is that it constitutes the great dissolution of the universe in an all-consuming fire at the end of an aeon. Destruction is a function of Time that in post-Vedic mythology causes the very word for Time, which is Kāla, to become a synonym for death the destroyer, and a designation for Yama as ruler of the underworld, who carries as his principal attribute in the iconography a noose with which to ensnare the spirit of a victim and abstract it from his body.

By the time of the Upanishads Indian thinkers had had to face the antinomy of time, whose beginning and end are inconceivable, yet for which a lack of a beginning and an end is unacceptable. In the Atharva Veda hymns cited above, the answer was given in simple terms that Time is all-inclusive and rolls on endlessly, but in the passage quoted from the Maitri Upanishad, the antinomy was resolved by asserting that the Absolute, which is Brahman, is beyond Time, is in fact the Timeless, just as elsewhere the Absolute is beyond space and beyond the unending regressus of effect and cause. Time therefore remains, as the Rig Veda puts it, a wheel that revolves ceaselessly; it is measured by the sun, which passes above the recumbent earth, constantly pursuing its ordered round among the asterisms by which time is measured, in each annual revolution following the identical course which it followed in the preceding revolutions and, prophetically speaking, will follow in its revolutions to come.

The idea of the cycle of time is greatly elaborated in both Jainism and Buddhism and also in Hinduism. Which environment first developed its own complex later form we cannot say; possibly all were elaborating the idea simultaneously; for time is frequently mentioned and described in greater or less detail in various places in the older works of Jainism and Buddhism and in the Mahabhārata, the lawbook of Manu, and other Hindu texts.

In Jainism the idea took the form of an elaboration of the Wheel of Time (*kālacakra*). This, say the Jains, has twelve spokes (*ara*), and the twelve divisions of the wheel made by them are six in a sequence of progressively ascending evolution (*utsarpiṇī*), when conditions in the world are steadily improving, while the other six are in a descending devolution (*avasarpiṇā*), when conditions in the world are steadily deteriorating. We saw at the beginning of this lecture something of the character of the advance and the retrogression of the world in these two processes. The six parts of the wheel which constitute the devolution always begin with a period which is doubly good (*suṣamasuṣamā*); this is followed by a period which is only good (*suṣamā*). Then comes a period which is prevailingly good but is mixed with evil (*suṣamaduḥṣamā*), after which comes a period which is prevailingly evil but mixed with good (*duḥṣamasuṣamā*). The next to last period is only evil (*duḥṣamā*), while the last is doubly evil (*duḥṣamaduḥṣamā*). When the bottom of the devolution is reached, the process is reversed, and the ascent starts with the doubly evil and period by period continues to the doubly good. The length of time that elapses for a full cycle of all twelve parts of the wheel involves some superastronomical calculations. It amounts to twenty *koṭākoṭīs* of *sāgaropamas* of *palyopamas,* that is, 20 x $10{,}000{,}000^2$ x 10 x $10{,}000{,}000^2$ of *palyopamas,* which could be represented, as I figure it, by two followed by thirty zeros of *palyopamas*. A *palyopama* is a measure of time, but how many years it contains is baffling for us to ascertain, and we must in part do our own estimating. The Jains estimate it by such statements as that a *palyopama* contains as many years as would be required to empty a cylinder-shaped container four miles (one *yojana*) high and four miles in circumference, tightly packed with the finest of human body hairs, if every hundred years a single hair were abstracted from it.

The length of time covered by the six kinds of periods vary as do also the size of the human body and the duration of life. At the beginning of the present half-cycle in the doubly good period, human beings were six miles tall and lived for three *palyopamas*. By the end of the fourth period in the downward course and the beginning of the fifth period, which is that in which we are now living, maximum human stature had shrunk to seven cubits (*hasta*), about ten and one-half feet, and maximum span of life had shortened to a hundred years. By the time the sixth period is concluded, some 39,000 years from now, stature will have been reduced to one *hasta* (a foot and a half) and maximum life-span to sixteen years.

The world was morally good enough to get along without Saviors until the third period in the downward course was reached, that of good mixed with evil; then the first Savior (*tīrthaṃkara*) arose. He was followed by twenty-three other Saviors in that and the next period, which latter was that in which the world still had some good in it though outweighed by evil. The last Savior in the series, who was Mahāvīra, died shortly before that fourth period ended and the fifth period started, which is the present period, that of evil, and the world has since been too evil for a Savior to be born or even for anyone to win release from rebirth. It will be more than 80,000 years from now, when another period of evil mixed with good has been reached in the upward course, before anyone can achieve salvation.

This symmetrically designed progression of time expressed as an eternally operating self-winding mechanism, which proceeds by aeons of such length as to stagger the human imagination, an elaborate alternation of decline and rise enclosed in a geometrical figure, a circle, in which movement is continuous, with no starting point and no terminus, is the accepted Jain answer to the problem of time. Such is that faith's teaching concerning our part of the universe. But there are other parts where time stands still! That latter condition calls for different cosmological conceptions, which, however, do not really concern us world-dwelling mortals.

The Buddhist conception of the cycle of time is considerably different from that of Jainism, but it will not be described here. The Buddhists had much less interest in the question of time than did the Jains or the Hindus, since consideration of it, as of other kinds of metaphysical speculation, did not seem to them to conduce to an attack upon the central problem facing man, which they held was extinction of suffering. They did, however, think that existence has had no conceivable beginning, and they considered that time passed in aeons, called *kalpa,* of incalculable length. In commenting on the length of an aeon, the Buddha is represented in the Pali canon (Saṃyutta Nikāya 15:ii.178–193) as using a series of illustrations. I shall cite only one, which is that if there were a range of mountains a league in length, a league in breadth, a league in height, made of adamant, without a cleft or a crack, and once every hundred years an eagle were to fly across it with a silken streamer in its beak and were to swish the mountain just once with the streamer, the length of time that would be required for the mountain to waste away would be less than an aeon. This and the other illustrations in the series pertain only to one aeon, one cycle of time. But the number of cycles of time already passed is more than all the grains of sand from the source of the Ganges to its mouth, and as many may be expected in the future.

Though the Hindu religious and philosophical texts have many variations in their views of time, they still have a degree of basic uniformity, and the teaching of the Purāṇas may be fairly cited as illustrative. The Purāṇas are texts compiled during a period starting probably at around the fourth or fifth century of our era and continuing for many hundreds of years. The Puranic conception of time is the most widely accepted among tradition-minded Hindus today.[2] It may be expressed in the form of a table, as follows:

1 human year	=	1 day and night of the gods
360 human years	=	1 year of the gods, that is, divine year
12,000 divine years (4,320,000 human years)	=	1 four-age period (caturyuga) or great period (*mahāyuga*) composed as follows:

1. Kṛta or Kṛtayuga, the golden age, named after the side of a rectangular, or long, die marked with four dots, consisting of 1,440,000 human years, plus a dawn and a twilight each of 144,000 human years, giving a total of 1,728,000 years.
2. Tretā or Tretāyuga, the silver age, named after the side of the die marked with three dots, consisting of 1,080,000 human years, plus a dawn and a twilight each of 108,000 human years, giving a total of 1,296,000 years.
3. Dvāpara or Dvāparayuga, the copper age, named after the side of the die marked with two dots, consisting of 720,000 human years, plus a dawn and a twilight each of 72,000 human years, giving a total of 864,000 years.

4. Kali or Kaliyuga, the iron age, named after the side of the die marked with one spot, consisting of 360,000 human years, plus a dawn and a twilight each of 36,000 human years, giving a total of 432,000 years.

1,000 four-age periods = 1 day of Brahmā or a Kalpa. Creation takes place and lasts during Brahmā's day; at its close the worlds are dissolved for the same length of time, which is his night. 360 such days and nights = one year of Brahmā. 100 such years = Brahmā's life span.

Also, one day of Brahmā = 14 *manvantaras*. A *manvantara* is a period of a Manu, and a Manu is the mythical progenitor of the world in his period, a kind of secondary creator who exercises the functions of a regent of the world throughout his *manvantara.*

One *manvantara* = 71 four-age periods (a *caturyuga*), with a surplus. One *manvantara* succeeds another. When a manvantara comes to an end, there is a relatively short period in which life ceases in the world, and at that time the Manus (regents of the *manvantaras*) with the minor gods (who are all the gods except Brahmā, Vishnu, and Shiva), the seven sages (*ṛṣis*), and the forefathers ascend to a higher sphere, to remain for a Kṛta period to preserve life. Then they resume activities as new persons with new names, introducing the next *manvantara* and restoring life to the world. At the end of the fourteenth *manvantara* comes the great dissolution (*naimittika prasarga*), and all is dissolved and remains so while Brahmā sleeps upon the great ocean, where, according to the texts, the seven sages (*ṛṣis*) watch over his slumber. The souls at this time rest from their wandering. When Brahmā wakes, the world is recreated and the souls resume their wandering.

Brahmā is now in the first *kalpa* of his fifty-first year. Six Manus of that *kalpa* have passed away. We are living in the Kaliyuga of the twenty-eighth four-age period (*caturyuga*) of the seventh *manvantara* of Brahmā's fifty-first year. The Kaliyuga began on February 18, 3102 B.C. This would seem to indicate that we have a little less than 426,933 years to go until the Kaliyuga with its twilight comes to an end, and we have to face dissolution!

The various Jain, Buddhist, and Hindu notions of the cycle of time would be only curious examples of ingenious systematization and arithmetical calculation, barren academic exercises, were they not associated with certain religious and ethical notions which have been accepted in all three faiths as axiomatic and have a powerful grip upon the popular mind.

The first of these is the joint doctrine of rebirth and *karma*. Death does not terminate one's existence. All it does is to initiate a new existence, the conditions of which are determined by one's actions in previous existences. The number of existences in this repeated continuation is incalculable; as the Buddhists put it, rebirth has no conceivable beginning (Pali *anamatagga*), and the other faiths agree. It has operated throughout all time. Only the very rarest person has learned ultimate truth, realized man's identity with the Absolute, however the Absolute is conceived, and so escaped from transmigration, but the rest of living creatures are still caught in the continuous process. The thought of the unnumbered, in fact the innumerable existences each one of us has experienced in the innumerable billions of years embraced by the past, and the expectation of an equally incalculable number of new existences in an equally incalculable number of billions of years in the future, is a grim, disheartening, terrifying prospect. It is a prospect of perpetual motion with never a moment of rest. The commonest word in India for the process is *saṃsāra,* which means "the wandering." It is endless movement, in which no one has the same companion for more than an infinitesimal fraction of his existences; he is solitary, unfriended, solely reliant upon himself. He cannot even count upon retaining some advance he has made upward on the way to release, for every action he performs has an inevitable effect, whether for good or ill, and a slip from the upward course may cause him to fall back with all the hard climbing to be repeated. Man has made his own past and his own present—no one has made it for him—and he is now making his own future. When he dies, his deeds are totalled up mechanically as in an equation handled in a cosmic computer, and the result leads him "alone" to enter "the mortal gate of the city, which he painted with shunless destiny."

Sooner or later every deed's effect must be felt by the doer of it. As a Sanskrit proverb puts it: It may be a day, or a week, or a month, or a year, or another life, but the effect of one's actions must at some time be experienced. Nothing is ever forgiven. A sin may be punished in this present life. Or, on the other hand, many existences may intervene before the result of the action matures. The Jain, the Buddhist, and the Hindu Scriptures all record many such cases. For example, when Mahāvīra had come almost to the end of his quest for full and complete knowledge, he was in a forest engaged in ascetic meditation. Certain *karma* which he had accumulated in a previous existence by pouring melted tin in another person's ears, had come to the point of ripening. His victim had been reborn in a village nearby as a cowherd, who at this time had let his bulls loose outside the village, while he went to milk the cows. The bulls wandered away. The cowherd came seeking them and chanced upon Mahāvīra. He asked Mahāvīra if he had seen the bulls, but Mahāvīra was too deeply absorbed in his meditation to hear him. "Sir, where are my bulls? Why don't you answer me, you monkling? Don't you hear? Or are your earholes useless?" When Mahāvīra still did not reply, the cowherd in a blind fury took two spikes and drove them into Mahāvīra's ears until they met inside his head and became one. He then cut off the protruding ends so that no one might see them and draw the spikes out. After that he left. When Mahāvīra had finished his meditation, he went to a nearby village and entered the house of a merchant to break his fast. A physician was there, who by his unusual insight recognized Mahāvīra's true character and acclaimed him for his fortitude in carrying arrows in his body. The merchant was doubtful, but the physician pointed out the spikes in Mahāvīra's ears. While the two were discussing the matter, Mahāvīra went outside the village to a grove, where he engaged in pious meditation. The merchant and the physician hastened after him with medical appurtenances. They bathed him with a vessel of oil and had powerful shampooers rub him. Under the shampooing Mahāvīra's joints were all loosened, and with them the spikes fell apart inside his head like a pair of tongs coming open, and out they dropped from his earholes covered with blood. At the same time the *karma* came out. The pain was so great that Mahāvīra emitted a mighty cry like that of a mountain struck by a thunderbolt, which would have burst the earth had he not taken care to save it. The merchant and the physician asked and received forgiveness for causing Mahāvīra pain, and went home. Although they had caused him pain, they had acted with good intentions, and in return they were reborn in heaven as gods. But the cowherd was reborn in the seventh hell.[3]

Good deeds also may have a delayed or cumulative effect, as in the case of the Buddha. Through many previous existences, the legends tell us, he had practised the virtue of alms-giving or generosity, which is the first of the Buddhist Ten Perfections. The instances of his generosity are sometimes incredible, as when he was born as the Prince Vessantara, whom the late Professor A. Foucher called a monomaniac of charity, for Vessantara gave away to beggars all his own and the state's possessions and even his wife and his children and finally his own life.

Again some small act of charity may bring a great reward. A touching and popular episode is that of a child who offered to the Buddha the only gift he could make, which was a handful of dust, which the Buddha received and then prophesied that in a future birth the child would become a great king. Legend has it that he became the emperor Ashoka.

To believe in the inevitable sequence of rebirth in the ceaseless cycle of existences, that unlimited renewal of becomings, which are as infinite in number as the reflections of an object placed between two facing mirrors, is joined the idea that existence is essentially composed of suffering. The Buddha declared this in his first sermon, making it the first of the Four Noble Truths which he enunciated to the five monks who were his audience.

> This, O monks, is the noble truth of suffering. Birth is suffering; old age is suffering; illness is suffering; death is suffering; association with what one dislikes is suffering; separation from what one likes is suffering; not to get what one wants is suffering—in short all the five-fold attachment to existence is suffering.

The underlying cause of the suffering is desire. This we saw is an idea appearing in the Upanishads, where the seeker of the highest knowledge must have only that knowledge, only Brahman, as his desire. All other desires must be extinguished, for they constitute attachment to the Unreal and are therefore profitless and impede the search for the Real. In the Bhagavad Gītā a similar teaching appears when Krishna tells Arjuna that he must refrain from action and adopt inaction. But inaction does not consist of no action, for everyone must perform acts, but it consists of doing them only because they are one's duty. Inaction consists of acting selflessly (BG 4.19–23). The Buddha developed a similar idea in the second and third of the Four Noble Truths.

> This, O monks, is the noble truth of the origin of suffering. It is that craving which leads to rebirth, joining itself to pleasure and lust, finding delight now here, now there—the craving for sensual pleasures, the craving for existence, the craving for wealth and power.
>
> This, O monks, is the noble truth concerning the cessation of suffering. It is the complete extinction without remainder of that craving, the giving up of it, the loosing of its hold, emancipation from it, release from it, doing away with it.

The most critical time in connection with desire is the hour of death. Whatever one fixes his mind on then is likely to determine his future state, for he is thought to fix his mind in his last moment on that which expresses his deepest desire. The Bhagavad Gītā makes this point emphatically: whoever meditates on Me (Krishna) alone at the hour of his death, goes to My (Krishna's) estate (BG 8.5; cf. 8.10; 8.13).[4] There are many stories in Indian literature exploiting this motif. A small folktale expresses it succinctly. As a man lay dying, a friend plucked a rose and held it before his eyes, and the man fixed his gaze on it and, holding it so fixed, died. The friend then asked a holy man standing there what was the state in which his friend had been reborn. "Let me show you," answered the holy man. He took the rose, parted the petals, and saying "There is your friend," pointed to a small insect lying in the rose's heart.

The sufferings of a single person in the passage through his many existences are beyond description. The late E. W. Burlingame, summarizing a long Pali passage on this theme in which the Buddha is speaking to his monks, puts it: "The bones left by a single individual in his passage from birth to birth, during a single cycle of time would form a pile so huge that were all the mountains of Vepulla-range to be gathered up and piled in a heap, that heap of mountains would appear as naught beside it. The head of every man has been cut off so many times in his previous states of existence, either as a human being or as an animal, as to cause him to shed blood more abundant than all the water contained in the four great oceans. For so long a time as this, you have endured suffering, you have endured agony, you have endured calamity. In view of this you have every reason to feel disgust and aversion for all existing things and to free yourselves from them." [5]

An inescapable feature of the doctrine of rebirth is the fact of impermanence. Nothing endures. Even though one is born as a god and as such enjoys the maximum of pleasure for a billion or more years, the state is not permanent and sooner or later he will fall to be reborn as a human being, an animal, even a victim in hell with its dreadful and ingenious punishments. This impermanence clouds all joy, which can in consequence be only momentary. Doom—and it is doom of an unknown character—is always just around the corner.

To compound all this aggregate of misery is a widespread belief that it is only in an existence as a human being that one performs acts which have a result, whether for good or ill. Animals cannot accumulate merit (*puṇya*) or demerit (*pāpa*); neither can residents of heaven (gods or their attendants) nor residents of hell. They are merely paying up for evil *karma* which they performed, it may be hundreds of existences before, or reaping the reward of good acts also performed then, or experiencing both the good and evil effects. A being's only chance to improve himself—or to injure himself—is when born as a human being. But unfortunately human birth is hard to obtain. The Jains say that the congruence of circumstances and qualities resulting in human birth is as rare as if the yoke of a bullock cart and its yokepin were separated and thrown into the ocean, where they would be blown about by the winds and tossed about by the waves and sent in diverse directions by the currents, but at last by some chance would be reunited and the yokepin should find its place again in the yoke. So difficult is it, say the Jain monks, to gain birth as a human being, and when one does gain it, he should grasp the opportunity it affords and utilize it to the full.

Such is man's position in the cycle of time. Rebirth, the effect of *karma,* the misery of existence, the need for final transcendental knowledge in order to escape from the cycle present him with a problem that on practical grounds seems insoluble and can lead only to a sequence of rebirths that appear as endless as the numerals that stretch out to the right of the decimal point when one tries to find an exact value for Pi. This is the theoretical ground of Indian pessimism. Yet there is a universal Indian belief that there is hope, that the hold of Time's noose can be broken, that an escape from the *saṃsāra,* the round of transmigration, is possible. Great souls, great teachers have found the answer and proclaimed it. That achievement is to be the subject of the final lecture in this series.

4.
The Conquerors

When the Aryans first entered India, probably at around 1500–1200 B.C., life may have seemed complicated and difficult to them, but it was far less so than it was to seem seven hundred to a thousand years later in the fifth century B.C. when Jainism and Buddhism were being preached and Hinduism was taking its classical form. In fact, life in the early Vedic period might have been looked upon in retrospect as relatively simple. Man did not then have to contend with anything but the immediate tangible world as he conceived it. All that he imagined his world to be was the here and now. He had the problems of making a living, struggling against disease, contending with enemies, getting and raising an abundant progeny to guarantee his lineage, adjusting to his family and neighbors and rulers. There were, indeed, some other beings to deal with whom he did not see (at least not in normal circumstances)—gods and demons—but these, too, were not outside his environment. The gods attended the sacrifices he offered if the priests officiating in his behalf invoked them with the correct ritual and he had made acceptable offerings. These gods sat on the straw spread for them in the sacrificial enclosure, and Agni, god of the sacrificial fire, carried to them the oblations which had been poured in the fire. Though the gods were invisible to all but the eye of faith, the sacrificer knew that they were present. Demons, too, were present, equally invisible to human eyesight but ready to pounce upon unwary mortals who slipped from the line of duty and destroy them; but by exercising reasonable precautions, using well-tried charms or other devices known by experience to be effective, a foresighted man could keep them off. The gods and the demons were understandable beings, moved by desires and passions akin to those that influence human behavior, not likely to develop caprices which a careful man could not anticipate. It was after all a fairly simple universe in which he lived, and he knew how to deal with it.

But by seven hundred to a thousand years later the universe had altered profoundly and in ways that left man baffled and helpless. The metaphysicians, not content to let that early simple world alone, had been inquiring and speculating about it. They had decided that it could not have come into existence as the result of conflict between a mighty, divine, benevolent hero demiurge named Indra, promoting progress and righteousness, who had slain an evil, monstrous dragon that was holding in confinement the heavenly waters and life-giving sun and frustrating the establishment of a code of cosmic law which the world needed for its successful operation. Indra and the gods allied with him had been repudiated. First they had been superseded by an over-god, a superdeity. But the latter, too, had been displaced, in his case by some first principle, primal cause, with no human emotions, neuter and not accessible to any human appeal, a gigantic mechanism operating in a completely impersonal way, no respecter of persons however persuasive they might be. Common sense had given way to an involved rationalism that had paradoxically led to a transcendentalism which the ordinary man could not conceive, let alone comprehend.

Also, man had lost the comfortable and delightful prospect of eternal life in a heaven well-stocked with all the joys of the immediate world. In its place he was now being assured that he had before him rebirth in some other form, probably no better than the existence which he was experiencing and liable to be a great deal worse, which would be followed by death again, then rebirth, then renewed death, after which would come another existence, and so on in an unending series, with each successive existence having an unpredictable character.

What is more, the men of learning had tampered with time. It had ceased to be the present, which had been preceded by a dimly conceived indefinite past and was to be followed by an equally dim and undefined future, a sequence which he did not worry about much. But now time had come to be viewed as beginningless and endless, stretching backward and forward without limit, beyond the capacity of the human mind to imagine. And man was caught in that resistless stream, noosed by relentless death, which led him on in a never-ending series of existences, all of them filled with suffering even for those beings that seemed fortunate. For no one of the existences was permanent but was bound to come to an end, and the happier any one condition might seem to be, the greater the misery arising from its inevitable termination.

To complicate the situation man had come to believe that the animal world he saw about him and the heavenly beings and hell-dwellers whom he could not see were all in the same cycle of rebirth as he was. He himself had had such forms countless times in the past and could expect to have them countless times in the future. And they, for their part, had probably all been human beings many times and doubtless would be again. He and they were all enmeshed in the saṃsāra, the wandering in many forms throughout the universe. He should have a feeling of compassion for them as well as for his fellow human creatures. Especially should he remember to have such a feeling for animals, less intelligent than he and so often at his mercy. He must practice noninjury toward them. If he did, he might hope to escape some of the misery of his impending future. If he did not, retribution was sure.

Such was man's predicament. He was living in a world that in an absolute sense was not real, yet was full of misery which he would experience for countless cycles of time, and all the rest of animate creation was in the same predicament. It was a ceaseless painful journey with no discernible resting-place.

"God offers to everyone his choice between truth and repose," says Emerson as quoted by Edith Hamilton. "Take which you please—you can never have both." Early Vedic man had expected to have both. But by the middle of the first millennium B.C. the speculative thinkers of India had set up and supported the proposition that man could get repose only if he denied phenomenal truth. He had to accept the idea that the universe as he saw it and was experiencing it was not the ultimately real universe. He had to penetrate behind it to find reality, which had none of the attributes, qualities, properties of the world he knew. To do so he had to rid himself of all human desires related to the phenomenal world, even the desire for family relationships, and have only the single desire of knowing and experiencing that solitary neuter principle which lies behind and, though unseen, permeates the multiple-seeming illusionary universe in which he saw himself. By so doing he could escape from unreality, from the noose of time, from rebirth, from misery.

And this he had to do for himself. No one could do more for him than give him the first impetus to enter upon the search for the Real, show him how to take the first step on a long and difficult way. Such a teacher was necessary, but he could not win salvation for the disciple, who was always the builder of his own future. Most people were left numb before the problem and gave it up. They took the attitude that success was beyond them. They might just as well do so and leave the effort to persons of greater intellectual capacity and strength of will. They greatly admired such persons, but for themselves they would be content with a modest effort, living by a simplified ethical code that would reduce evil *karma* and increase good, and so palliate the misery of future existences, though not cure it. They would placate the minor godlings of disease, childbearing, prosperity; worship the great gods who were confessedly not the Absolute; deal only with what they had the intelligence to grasp or the imagination to conceive. They would merely make the best of a situation that for all their practical purposes was hopeless.

It was no wonder that the Upanishadic teachers never made an effort to preach their theories to the population at large, for they knew the effort would not succeed. Only those rare persons who had unusual mental endowment could comprehend their instruction, and among these only the still fewer of iron will could renounce the natural desires of mankind and undeviatingly concentrate on pursuit of the highest knowledge. Those thinkers' teachings were bound by the very facts of human limitation to remain esoteric. The teachers, therefore, sought no converts but adopted a life of seclusion as anchorites in the forest, where the few capable disciples whom they accepted could pursue the great quest. Their attitude was intellectually aristocratic, denying equality—snobbish, to use a pejorative word. They were not preaching a popular religion nor even trying to set up a school or a community.

But it was also no wonder that teachers who arose then with an attitude that something could be done for a less exclusively selected audience got a large following. The old Vedic sacrifice had gone bankrupt; its ritual had lost its meaning; while the Upanishadic anchorites were as inaccessible physically in their huts and caves as they were intellectually when, sunk in trance, they experienced their indescribable and incomprehensible Absolute and encouraged their few chosen acolytes to do likewise. But people of only moderate or less than moderate intelligence and power of will also wanted teachers—as the Upanishads themselves said a serious searcher must have (CU 6.14; Śvet 6.23; Maitri 6.28; Muṇḍ 1.2.12–13). They too were seeking someone to show them how to escape the *saṃsāra,* the continuous process of rebirth, of constant change into some new and different and all too often frightening and repulsive form.

Within the orthodox Brahmanic Hindu environment, such teaching was voiced in the Bhagavad Gītā, the religious lyric recited by Krishna, who was considered to be God incarnate. This text taught that man can win release in three ways. One of these was by fulfilling the old Vedic conception of duty, but with a modification; that is, he should look upon his duty as the performance of works, though not ritual works as prevailingly prescribed in the Veda, but rather the acts pertaining to his personal function in the cosmos, a concept which was intimated in the Rig Veda but not stressed. He should do such acts, not because of their consequences, their fruit, whether happy or painful. Specifically, he must not be beguiled by the attraction of the Vedic heaven, which is the goal of men moved by desire (2.43). The Vedas, the Gītā says here and elsewhere, do not teach the highest doctrine; they lead at best to a limited and impermanent state; they deal only with the material. One must learn to be above the pairs of opposites—good and evil, pain and pleasure, and others. One's mental attitude (*buddhi*) must be stabilized. He must engage in action (karma), for it is impossible not to do so, but he must have no interest in its fruits. This state is in no way to be reached by mere nonaction, that is, by refraining from action. It is by doing his duty selflessly that he achieves genuine inaction and is released from the bond of rebirth to reach that highest place, which is free from illness (*padaṃ gacchanty anāmayam* 2.51).

The second way to salvation which the Gītā teaches is that of knowledge. This is the rigorously intellectual method of the Upanishads, hard to achieve, won through meditation practiced in solitude, with the mind, the thought organ (*manas*) controlled, and in concentration on the self, which is one's real person and is also God. One who is so concentrated, says Krishna, "sees Me in all and all in Me" (6.30). The method is difficult because the thought organ is fickle and hard to control, but Krishna gives assurance that progress once made by this means is not lost, even in the following existences, until finally after a series of rebirths the man devoted to this arduous discipline wins the highest goal (*yāti parāṃ gatim* 6.45).

The third way enunciated by Krishna is the high point of the Gītā's teaching. This is the doctrine of Bhakti, "loving devotion" to God. When Arjuna, to whom Krishna was reciting the Gītā, asked Krishna to reveal himself in his godhead, Krishna did so and this transcendent view which Krishna gave of himself to Arjuna is the climax of the Gītā (chapter 11). Arjuna saw God in his supernal form, yet Arjuna had not mastered the way to God either by disciplined selfless action or by the way of knowledge. He had only declared himself a full believer (11.1) and had asked Krishna in his grace to reveal himself, and Krishna had done so. Hence Krishna said, after manifesting himself (11.52–54), that by unswerving devotion one can come to see him and then added a stanza that to this day carries hope to Hindus: "whoever does My work, intent on Me, with devotion to Me, free from attachment, without enmity to any creature, he goes to Me" (11.55). The simple but devout heart is enough. By means of it one can gain the fullest knowledge through God's grace, can know God, can win to God. Such a one has, in fact, a special advantage. "I am the same to all beings," says Krishna, "there is no one either hateful to Me or dear; but those who adore Me with loving devotion, they are in Me and I too in them" (9.29). "Blessed are the pure in heart; for they shall see God"—this thought, whether in India or in Palestine, has won the hearts of men.

Besides devotees of Krishna, who is an incarnation of the god Vishnu, Hinduism knows devotees of other deities, the god Shiva and his wife Pārvatī. The latter is the Great Mother, compassionate to creatures, the feminine Savior who rescues from destruction and misery, the female principle that gives life and movement to the universe, Devī, the goddess, in whom the whole universe is contained. Says a poet in a widely used ode to her (Saundaryalaharī 4, 22, 27):

4

Other than you the host of gods grant freedom from danger and gifts with their hands;
You alone make no overt gesture of gift and immunity;
for to save from danger and to grant a reward even beyond desire,

O you who are the refuge of the worlds, your two feet alone are adequate.

22

"Do you, O lady, extend to me, your slave, a compassionate glance!"—
When one desiring to praise you utters the words, "you, O lady" [*bhavāni tvam,* which words also mean "May I be you!"],
at that moment you grant him a state of identity with you,
with your feet illuminated by the crests of [the great gods] Vishnu, Brahmā, and Indra [lying prostrate before you in worship].

Hence the poet prays:

27

Let my idle chatter be the muttering of prayer, my every manual movement the execution of ritual gesture,
my walking a ceremonial circumambulation, my eating and other acts the rite of sacrifice,
my lying down prostration in worship, my every pleasure enjoyed with dedication of myself,
let whatever activity is mine be some form of worship of you.

When a devout Hindu resorts to Krishna (or Vishnu) or to Shiva or to Devī, he is addressing a supreme personal deity, with whom he can expect to make contact. The deity can hear him, consider his prayer, grant him favor. But it is not possible to do this under a system which finds the Absolute in a neuter first principle or a cosmic mechanism operating impersonally, inexorably, subject to no appeal, knowing neither compassion nor anger, showing no forgiveness, forgetting nothing, whether good or evil, practising neither injustice nor justice, acting neither morally nor immorally, but going on its course like the wind in the atmosphere or the stars in the heavens.

There are other systems, namely Jainism and Buddhism, which contain a still larger human element. They are not systems proclaimed by a diety or centered on a deity whose human element is merely an accessory to his divinity rather than an essential element. They are instead systems discovered or framed and then promulgated by human teachers, who did not look upon mankind from outside or from above but were themselves a part of humanity born to the same plight and misery that all humanity faces. These teachers conquered the misery, found an escape from rebirth, and then, their hearts filled with pity for their suffering fellows, became evangelists, touring the part of India where they lived, preaching the good tidings to all who wished to hear, and they instructed their disciples too to spread the good tidings abroad. The founders' message was aided by the fact that they were not high priests "which cannot be touched with the feeling of our infirmities" but were "in all points tempted like as we are." Since they as human beings overcame the obstacles to salvation, there is hope for all men that they, too, may succeed. We mortals should revere them, study their teachings, follow them, imitate them. Such is the belief. Even though we and they cannot now communicate, we can gain courage and strength from contemplating the victory they won. Hence the value of images or idols of these teachers, which help us to visualize them.

Legend clusters around these figures, and the bare skeleton of fact which we have concerning them is filled out and enriched with marvels accompanying their conception, birth, infancy, boyhood, the hardships they endured from demonic attacks, tales of wonders worked, benevolence and compassion practiced, infinite knowledge demonstrated. The myth far outweighs fact and is vastly more important to their followers.[1] Thus the total body of fact and myth becomes man's refuge, his hope-instilling example of salvation. He cannot obtain his salvation from their efforts; he must win it by his own unremitting toil in the great quest, but now, in viewing these teachers' victory, he has the certainty that the hope which moves him is not a blind one but can come true. The triumph those conquerors won they won for all future generations.

Jainism, the older of these two evangelical faiths, is considered to have been founded by Pārshva (*pārśva*) and two and one-half centuries later to have been widely preached by Mahāvīra. Buddhism was taught by Siddhārtha Gautama. With respect to Pārshva our documented information is absolutely minimal. He is said by Jain tradition to have lived for a hundred years and to have died two hundred and fifty years before Mahāvīra did. This latter event the Jain tradition sets at a date corresponding to 528 B.C., but modern western scholarship sets it at 487 or 477 B.C. This would put Pārshva's death at 737 or 727 B.C. He would have been living early in the Upanishadic period, while Mahāvīra would have been living in the middle or latter part of that period. Pārshva enjoined upon his monastic followers four vows: noninjury of living creatures (*ahiṃsā*), truthfulness, the taking of only what one has been given, and the possession of no property (except for the usual monkish accoutrements of begging bowl, broom, and others). Mahāvīra enjoined upon his disciples five vows, the four prescribed by Pārshva and a fifth, that of celibacy. Pārshva allowed his disciples an upper and a lower garment, but Mahāvīra allowed none. The common Jain tradition is that Pārshva and Mahāvīra founded two separate orders, which were united when the head of Pārshva's order and Mahāvīra's chief disciple chanced to meet, discussed doctrinal matters, and found themselves in agreement on all points including Mahāvīra's fifth vow, that of celibacy. Though this was not explicitly stated in Pārshva's list of vows, it was considered to be implicit in his fourth vow, that of nonpossession of property, for that included nonpossession of a woman. The two orders then united, though the issue of clothing was not settled, and to this day the Jain community is split in two divisions—the Shvetāmbaras, whose monks wear only white clothing, and the Digambaras, whose monks wear no clothing except the sky.

Mahāvīra's father, we are told, was a petty raja in Bihar in northern India. He died when Mahāvīra was thirty years old, whereupon Mahāvīra, who had promised not to leave his parents as long as they were alive, turned to the religious life. He took a year to give away his property and arrange his affairs, and then became a mendicant wanderer. Thirteen months later, in the cold season, which can be very uncomfortable in Bihar, he dispensed with clothes. After intensive practice of severe austerities he finally won complete knowledge. He spent the rest of his life preaching his newly-found doctrine throughout Bihar and nearby and died at the age of seventy-two, forty-two years after becoming a monk. The texts say that thus he won final release from rebirth and his soul is now at that place at the top of the universe (*īṣātprāgbhāra*) reserved for the Perfected Beings (*siddha*).

The historical elements in the Buddha story are also probably very few and not very dramatic. Siddhārtha Gautama, the Buddha, was the son of a petty king in northern India near the present border with Nepal, and at the age of twenty-nine left home to enter upon the religious life. He first went to two honored teachers of his time, but he found them unable to help him win complete knowledge. Then with five disciples or companions he practised extreme asceticism, similar in general to that practised by Mahāvīra, so that his body wasted away to appalling meagerness and he nearly died, but this too he finally discontinued as profitless. He now ate normally, and without any external guidance passed from stage to stage of knowledge until at last, as he sat in trance under the great tree of enlightenment (*bodhi*), he finally won complete knowledge. Thus he became the Buddha, a title which means "the Enlightened One." Once he had won this victory, he returned to proclaim it to the five disciples, who are pictured as filled with scorn when they saw him approaching, because he had not been able to endure the rigors of the austerity which he had shared with them and then forsaken, while they had continued steadfast. But such a splendor emanated from him that they could not hold to their resolution to ignore him, and involuntarily they arose to greet him. There in a deer park at Sarnath outside Banaras (Varanasi) he preached his first sermon about the Four Noble Truths concerning misery, its origin, its cessation, and the way to achieve that cessation. This last is the noble eightfold path that avoids the extreme of sensual pleasures and the extreme of bodily mortification, and instead follows a middle course between them. Thus he set the wheel of the law rolling, and the five listeners became his first disciples. From then on he preached continuously throughout the eastern part of the present state of Uttar Pradesh and in Bihar until he died at the age of eighty. He had won Nirvāṇa long before, but that state of freedom from desire and from rebirth, of attainment of unalloyed bliss, was made permanent only on his death.

Both Mahāvīra and the Buddha were aided in their mission by the social conditions of the area in which they lived and preached. This area in the sixth century B.C. was only imperfectly Aryanized. The Brahmanic religion centered about the Vedic sacrifice was losing its prestige in its homeland in the Panjab and in the western part of what is now Uttar Pradesh, and the new ideas expressed in the Upanishads were being discussed in intellectual circles throughout the entire Aryan area including eastern Uttar Pradesh and Bihar. In that latter region, where the Brahman priesthood was a relatively new thing and had not fully established itself, commerce was developing and large cities were coming into existence. Trade routes had opened up eastward to the Bay of Bengal, and westward along the Ganges system to the Panjab and thence to Peshawar and on into Central Asia, Iran, and the West, while a branch route led off from it to the south and the seaports in Gujarat on the Arabian Sea. Such an expanding economy brought into existence in the cities a wealthy merchant class, which was not composed of priestly Brahmans but of Vaishyas, the merchant and artisan sector of society. At the same time in the rural regions of the area a wealthy landowning aristocracy had evolved, which as such was a noble or ruling class (*kṣatriya*) group. Both the landed nobility and the rich merchant class were restive at Brahman pretensions to moral and social superiority and were ready for the ministrations of such movements as Jainism and Buddhism, which repudiated Brahmanism on intellectual and religious grounds. The converts to the two new faiths, then, were prevailingly drawn from the rural landowners and the urban merchants. Jainism and Buddhism not only offered a solution to the problem of man's destiny in the universe but at the same time affirmed the worth of the Kshatriya and Vaishya segments of society, the lay nobility and wealthy middle class, against Brahmanic arrogance.

Much of the beauty and attraction of Janism and Buddhism lie in their golden legends of the life and acts of the founders—the conception, the birth, the infancy, the miracles—but we cannot pause here to recount these legends.

Mahāvīra's struggle to obtain complete enlightenment was one of extreme and never-ceasing austerity until he finally gained perfect knowledge. Thereupon the gods prepared a place for his first sermon, cleansing the ground for the space of a league (*yojana*) and scenting and ornamenting it. They erected three walls, the innermost being of jewels, the next of gold, and the third of silver, each wall having four gates facing the four directions. In the center was a tree under which were four lion thrones, also facing in the four directions. Mahāvīra sat on that facing east; replicas of him sat on the others. There he preached his first sermon, addressing an audience consisting of men, gods, and animals. After this, he set out on his long preaching mission, establishing a fourfold congregation of monks, nuns, laymen, and laywomen. When he died, legend says, the eighteen confederated kings of the time instituted an illumination on that day, which was a fast day. This festival was called Dīpāvalī (modern Hindi *dīvālī*), which means "row of lights." The king said, "Since the light of holy knowledge is gone, let us make a material illumination!" Mahāvīra's soul is now, of course, outside our universe, in the abode of the perfected (*siddhaśilā*).

Siddhārtha's career was quite different. The legends say that as a future Buddha he had through innumerable existences been acquiring the Ten Perfections. These are the perfections of almsgiving (generosity), keeping of the Buddhist precepts, renunciation, knowledge, courage, patience, truth, resolution, good will, indifference. He fulfilled these in all respects, and in fulfilling almsgiving he had in one of his previous existences (Vessantara) even made a gift of his own life, thus causing the earth to shake and quake seven times. Siddhārtha's final struggle to win enlightenment was a severe one. When he sat down under the Bodhi tree where he was to win it, he made a resolution not to leave the spot until he was successful. At this Māra, the Evil One, realizing that his sway over the world would end if Siddhārtha won supreme and absolute wisdom, summoned his army, mounted his elephant, which was one hundred and fifty leagues tall, and set out to attack him. The gods who were praising Siddhārtha fled as Māra approached. Then Māra attacked successively with a whirlwind, a great rain storm from clouds of a thousand strata that raised floods over the tops of the forest trees, then a shower of rocks, a shower of weapons, a shower of live coals, a shower of hot ashes, a shower of sand, a shower of mud, and a great darkness—all to no avail. He ordered Siddhārtha to surrender his seat to him, but Siddhārtha refused, telling him that he (Māra) had not fulfilled the Ten Perfections in even the lowest grade. Māra hurled his discus, but it turned into a canopy of flowers. Some of the texts enlarge the attacks by attributing to Māra the use of his daughters, lovely beyond dream, who employed every variety of feminine seduction to shake Siddhārtha's resolve, but again without success. Then Siddhārtha said to Māra, "Who is your witness to almsgiving?" Māra pointed to his army, from which came a roar, "I am his witness! I am his witness!" like the roar of an earthquake. Māra then asked Siddhārtha who was his witness, and the Buddha stretched out his arm to the mighty earth, asking it to bear witness that in his existence as Vessantara he had given a great seven-hundredfold alms. And in reply the mighty earth thundered "I am your witness!" emitting a hundred, a thousand, a hundred thousand roars, as if to overwhelm Māra's army. Māra and his army fled, and Siddhārtha was left free to continue to his final Enlightenment. The dramatic attack and defeat of Māra and his army is the most frequently represented scene in Buddhist iconography, showing the seated Buddha with hand touching the earth as he calls it to witness. Later Māra tried again to tempt the Buddha not to preach but to enter final Nirvāṇa at once, but again the Buddha sent him away defeated and dejected.

Like Mahāvīra the Buddha conducted a long preaching career and established a fourfold congregation, which hardly exists today in India but is known in various forms in Ceylon, Southeast Asia, Nepal, Central Asia, and East Asia. Buddhism, unlike Jainism, has been a great missionary religion, widespread outside the land of its origin, in this respect resembling Christianity.

The great conquerors, like victorious generals, had each a strategy for coping with man's problem in the universe. We may illustrate that fact in relation to the Buddha, as the Buddhist scriptures present him, and consider the colloquy between him and one of his disciples named Mālunkyāputta as recorded in a Pali text.[2] This disciple was one day meditating in seclusion when a thought occurred to him, as follows: "These theories which The Blessed One has left unelucidated, has set aside and ignored—that the world is eternal, that the world is not eternal; that the world is finite, that the world is infinite; that the soul and the body are identical, that the soul is one thing and the body another; that the saint exists after death, that the saint does not exist after death; that the saint both exists and does not exist after death, that the saint neither exists nor does not exist after death—these The Blessed One does not elucidate to me. And the fact the Blessed One does not elucidate them to me does not please me or suit me. Therefore I will draw near to The Blessed One and inquire of him concerning this matter. If The Blessed One will elucidate to me these points, in one way or another, in that case will I lead the religious life under

The Blessed One. But if he will not elucidate them to me, in that case will I abandon religious training and return to the lower life of a layman.

We can feel Mālunkyāputta's frustration as he thinks of this matter, and when he resorts to the Buddha, sets himself at one side, and presents the difficulty to him, we can almost hear his voice rising as he makes his complaint. He recites the list of problems, adding: "If The Blessed One knows the answers to these questions, then let him elucidate them to me. But if The Blessed One does not know the answers, then the only upright thing for one who does not know, or who has not that insight, is to say, 'I do not know; I have not that insight.' "

"Pray, Mālunkyāputta," said the Buddha, "did I ever say to you, 'Come, Mālunkyāputta, lead the religious life under me, and I will elucidate to you either that the world is eternal, or that the world is not eternal,' " and he went on to specify all the problems which Mālunkyāputta had raised.

"Nay, verily, Reverend Sir," Mālunkyāputta replied.

"Or did you ever say to me, 'Reverend Sir, I will lead the religious life under The Blessed One, on condition that The Blessed One elucidate to me either that the world is eternal, or that the world is not eternal,'' and so on.

"Nay, verily, Reverend Sir."

"That being the case, vain man, whom are you so angrily denouncing? Mālunkyāputta, any one who should say, 'I will not lead the religious life under The Blessed One until The Blessed One shall elucidate these questions to me—that person would die, Mālunkyāputta, before The Tathāgata had ever elucidated this to him.

"It is as if, Mālunkyāputta, a man had been wounded by an arrow thickly smeared with poison, and his friends and companions, his relatives and kinsfolk were to procure for him a physician or surgeon; and the sick man were to say, "I will not have this arrow taken out until I have learnt whether the man who wounded me was a kshatriya, or a Brahman, or a Vaishya, or a Shūdra; or until I have learnt his name and his clan; or whether he was tall or short or of medium height; or whether he was black or dusky or tawny; or whether he was from this village or that village or town or city; or whether the bow which wounded me was a *cāpa* or a *kodaṇḍa;* or whether the bowstring which wounded me was made from swallowwort or bamboo or sinew or *maruva* or milkweed; or whether the shaft which wounded me was a *kaccha* or a *ropima;* or whether the shaft which wounded me was feathered from the wings of a vulture or a heron or a falcon or a peacock or a *sithilahanu;* or whether the shaft which wounded me was wound round with the sinews of an ox or a buffalo or a *ruru* deer or a monkey; or whether the arrow which wounded me was an ordinary arrow or a clawheaded arrow or a *vekaṇḍa* or an iron arrow or a calftooth arrow or a *karavīrapatta.* That man would die, Mālunkyāputta, without ever having learnt this.

"In exactly the same way, Mālunkyāputta, any one who should say, 'I will not lead the religious life under The Blessed One until The Blessed One shall elucidate to me either that the world is eternal or that the world is not eternal' and all the other questions which you have raised—that person would die, Mālunkyāputta, before the Tathāgata had ever elucidated this to him.

"The religious life, Mālunkyāputta, does not depend on the dogma that the world is eternal or on the dogma that the world is not eternal, nor on any of the other dogmas which you have cited. Whichever alternatives among these pairs of dogmas obtain, there still remain birth, old age, death, sorrow, lamentation, misery, grief, and despair, for the extinction of which in the present life I am prescribing.

"Accordingly, Mālunkyāputta, bear always in mind what it is that I have not elucidated and what it is that I have elucidated. And what, Mālunkyāputta, have I not elucidated? I have not elucidated, Mālunkyāputta, that the world is eternal or not eternal, nor any of the other dogmas you have mentioned. And why, Mālunkyāputta, have I not elucidated this? Because, Mālunkyāputta, this profits not, nor has to do with the fundamentals of religion, nor tends to aversion, absence of passion, cessation, quiescence, the supernatural faculties, supreme wisdom, and Nirvāṇa; therefore have I not elucidated it.

"And what, Mālunkyāputta, have I elucidated? Misery, Mālunkyāputta, have I elucidated; the origin of misery have I elucidated; the cessation of misery have I elucidated; and the path leading to the cessation of misery have I elucidated. And why, Mālunkyāputta, have I elucidated this? Because Mālunkyāputta, this does profit, has to do with the fundamentals of religion, and tends to aversion, absence of passion, cessation, quiescence, knowledge, supreme wisdom, and Nirvāṇa; therefore have I elucidated it. Accordingly, Mālunkyāputta, bear always in mind what it is that I have not elucidated, and what it is that I have elucidated."

Thus spake The Blessed One; and, delighted, the venerable Mālunkyāputta applauded the speech of The Blessed One.

The Buddha in this way is represented as refusing to be sidetracked into those metaphysical questions which he considered irrelevant, as not tending to edification. He does not say he does not know the answers, and it would be unfair to think he was without opinions on them, for he was a thoughtful man, who is elsewhere described as given to rather involved chains of reasoning. But he had a message for the average mind, which could not comprehend philosophical subtleties, and by avoiding discussion of such subtleties he gave strength to that message.

Of the other teachers who showed a way to victory over the problem of rebirth and misery Krishna, as god, prescribed preferably loving devotion (*bhakti*) to himself; Mahāvīra prescribed a rigorous code of conduct with concentration upon the problem raised by *karma,* that is, motivated action, action with one's mind concerned with the consequences. With the Buddha the focus was on the elimination of suffering. All three teachers accepted the doctrine that man's predicament is related to the underlying reality of the universe, the result of action upon one's future condition, the unending round of rebirth in all kinds of bodies, the bondage of man and other creatures, who after all are his brothers, in the toils of time, but each focused his attack upon what he considered the critical spot in the whole terrifying complex of the universe. When the victory is won, joy, bliss beyond compare is the victor's reward. Thus, these teachers brought hope to humanity, which had become lost in confusion and fallen into despair before the perils of the universe which speculation had created. Men relied upon those teachers as Conquerors and Saviors and followed them as trusted leaders to the victory and reward which they now could see ahead. This was for them the Real and they could hope to attain it.

Notes

Introduction

1. Generally following H. C. Warren, *Buddhism in Translations,* in *Harvard Oriental Series,* Vol. III, Cambridge, Mass.: Harvard University Press, 1896, pp. 130–133.

2. Warren, *op. cit.,* pp. 237–238.

3. Warren, *op. cit.,* pp. 207–208.

Chapter 1. "The Search for the Real"

1. The following section of this lecture (pp. 17–22) is largely drawn from my article "The Creation Myth of the Rig Veda," *Journal of the American Oriental Society* LXII (1942), 85–98.

2. For translation of the Upanishads the reader is advised to use R. E. Hume, *The Thirteen Principal Upanishads,* 2d edition, revised, London, New York, and Madras: Oxford University Press, 1951.

3. For example, by Hume, *op. cit.,* pp. 23 ff.

Chapter 2. "The Unity of Life"

1. Franklin Edgerton, *Bhagavad Gītā, in Harvard Oriental Series,* Vol. 38–39, Cambridge, Mass.: Harvard University Press, 1944, part 2, p. 83. In the Harper Torchbooks paperbook edition (New York: Harper, 1964), the quotation appears on p. 185.

2. See E. W. Hopkins, *Ancient India,* in *Cambridge History of India,* Vol. I, edited by E. J. Rapson, Cambridge, England: University Press, 1922, p. 271.

3. See W. Norman Brown, "The Sanctity of the Cow in Hinduism," *Journal of the Madras University,* XXVIII (January, 1957), 29–49. This has been reprinted twice: (1) *Eco-*

nomic Weekly, Bombay, Annual Number (February, 1964), 245–255; (2) "La vache sacrée dans la religion hindoue," *Annales Economies Sociétés Civilisations,* Paris, No. 4 (1964), 643–664. For a full investigation of meat-eating in Hindu, Jain, and Buddhist texts, see the long and careful paper by Professor Ludwig Alsdorf, "Beiträge zur Geschichte von Vegetarismus und Rinderverehrung in Indien," *Abhandlungen der Geistes- und Sozialwissenschaftlichen Klassen,* Nr. 6 (1961), Akadamie der Wissenschaften und der Literatur in Mainz.

4. Mrs. C. A. F. Rhys Davids in *Cambridge History of India,* New York, The Macmillan Co., 1922, Vol. I, pp. 207, 215.

5. See Louis Renou, *Religions of Ancient India,* London: University of London, Athlone Press, 1953, p. 100.

6. J. N. Farquhar, *A Primer of Hinduism,* London and Madras: Oxford University Press, 1912, Sec. 115, p. 182.

7. In the discussion here of the sanctity and inviolability of the cow I have relied heavily upon my paper cited in n. 3, above.

8. See Maurice Bloomfield, *Religion of the Veda,* New York: Putnam, 1908, pp. 69 ff.

9. Maurice Bloomfield, *Hymns of the Atharva-Veda,* in *Sacred Books of the East,* edited by F. Max Müller, Oxford: Clarendon Press, 1897, Vol. 42, pp. 169–172, 174–179. Reprinted in Delhi: Banarsi Dass, 1964.

10. Ludwig Alsdorf., *op. cit.,* pp. 571, 589, 610: "sie (Ahiṃsā) hat ursprünglich mit Ethik in unserem Sinne nichts zu tun sondern ist ein magisch-ritualistiches Tabu auf das Leben, das in keiner seiner Formen zerstört werden darf" (p. 517).

Chapter 3. "Time Is a Noose"

1. Maurice Bloomfield, *Hymns of the Atharva-Veda* (cited *supra,* chap. 2, n. 9), pp. 224 ff.

2. The account here largely follows that of E. E. Pargiter in the *Encyclopedia of Religion and Ethics,* edited by James Hastings, New York, Scribner, 1908–27; 2d ed., 1951, Vol. 10, p. 447.

3. This story with a manuscript illustration appears in W. Norman Brown, *Miniature Paintings of the Jaina Kalpasūtra,* Washington, D.C.: Smithsonian Institution, 1934, p. 37 and fig. 77.

4. See Franklin Edgerton, "The Hour of Death," *Annals of the Bhandarkar Oriental Research Institute* (Poona), Vol.